CW00539362

THE
MIRACLE
HABITS

ALSO BY MITCH HOROWITZ

Occult America
One Simple Idea
The Miracle Club
Secrets of Self-Mastery
The Miracle of a Definite Chief Aim
The Power of the Master Mind
Magician of the Beautiful
Mind As Builder

THE
MIRACLE
HABITS

The Secret of Turning
Your Moments Into Miracles

Mitch Horowitz

author of *The Miracle Club*

MEDIA

MEDIA

Published 2020 by Gildan Media LLC
aka G&D Media
www.GandDmedia.com

First Edition: 2020

Front cover design by David Rheinhardt of Pyrographx
Cover photo by Larry Busacca

Interior design by Meghan Day Healey of Story Horse, LLC.

Library of Congress Cataloging-in-Publication Data is available upon request

ISBN: 978-1-7225-0230-0

10   9   8   7   6   5   4   3   2   1

To Jacqueline,
a miracle.

CONTENTS

INTRODUCTION

A PHILOSOPHY OF "CASH-VALUE"

have seen talented people squander promising careers, audiences, and prospects because they practiced bad habits in work and life. I have also watched people who appeared unexceptional attain notable success due to good habits.

But this book is about neither.

The Miracle Habits is about more than cultivating sanctioned notions of success or acceptance. It is not about being 10% happier, "good enough," or reorganizing your sock drawer. Rather, as the title implies, this book is about fostering miracles. Not as a once-in-a-lifetime experience but as a recurring and natural part of life. My definition of a miracle is simple: *a fortuitous event or circumstance that exceeds all conventional expectation.*

I believe in storming heaven—that is, in reaching unapologetically for the peak of what you want. Much of today's therapeutic and self-help talk of "purpose," "gratitude," and "meaning" is, in my view, misleading. Such terms are placeholders for the avoidance of naming what we really want in life. True purpose and meaning are found in personal power—in cultivated providence, epic performance, and ideal self-expression. Whatever your aims, needs, or wishes, *The Miracle Habits* demonstrates how to invite extraordinary (and ethical) possibilities into your life.

Be sure that you're in the right place: we are embarking on a path of attainment. As I've written in my previous book *The Miracle Club*, I believe that the contemporary seeker suffers from personal division and, ultimately, disappointment if he or she avoids the principle of accomplishment. I refuse to call aspirational wishes by terms like "identifications" or "attachments." These labels emerge from ancient and culturally conditioned religious traditions (all religions are culturally conditioned), which I consider poorly suited to much of modern life. Impulses of self-development and creativity dwell innately in your personhood. Honoring and ethically framing those impulses should be the aim of spirituality. By ethics I mean doing nothing to deny the self-development of another person that you seek for yourself. The friction you experience when deterred from creative impulses should be noticed—and heeded.

In early 2020, I heard from Colton Holmes of the Front Range area of Colorado.* Colton and his wife had recently left a spiritual community. Their former community offered them a familiar paradigm, which they came to question. He wrote me:

> We recently moved out of an ashram after eight years. I have struggled to let go of the ashram mentality that external things like money, retirement, and all of worldly existence essentially are only distractions and obstacles on a spiritual path. I personally feel, as I believe you do, that many of the old spiritual traditions need to take a good look at themselves. These traditional institutions teach in a way that supports the institutions themselves more than develops the students at a certain point.

I am in sympathy with that statement. And I take it further. I believe that you as a creative being—one said in spiritual traditions from Hermeticism to Judaism to be made in the image of the creator—*should* expect mira-

---

* Real names and locales appear with permission throughout this book. I discourage stories of "miracles" from untraceable or anonymous sources in some New Thought and inspirational literature. Truth requires transparency.

cles in your life. Although we face myriad complexities, and we experience multiple laws and forces, I believe that the song of self-expression, in its fullest and most varied sense, exists and yearns to spring forth from every person's psyche. Practices that curb that song produce inner conflict and frustration. I have witnessed too many colleagues on the spiritual path experience a terrible inner division between conditioned notions of non-attachment versus pursuit of their artistic, domestic, or financial wishes. Moreover, my experience, both personally and communally, is that the individual cannot be truly happy without singing the song of the self—without pursuing his or her deepest wishes, however defined. In matters of self-development, I see no division between depth and height, or spiritual and worldly to use general terms. The *manner* of your pursuit matters more than the *nature* of your pursuit. But it is vital that the individual find a path that most fully expresses the self, as he or she defines it.

Some spiritual traditions teach that we lack self-perspective and are too divided within to speak of possessing or understanding authentic wishes. Experience has taught me to dissent from that judgment. I believe that at certain sensitive moments, we, as individuals, possess higher perspective—not ultimate but higher. We are not the victims of a cosmic joke that deters us from knowing ourselves and what we truly wish for. Released from peer pressure and conditioning, we are more mature than we know.

The pushback against aspiration in both spiritual and literary culture can produce ironic and almost humorous results. In 2019, *The New York Times* op-ed page published an essay by a Princeton University writing instructor arguing against the "desire for greatness" and extoling the value of being "good enough." This is an increasingly popular theme among social critics, including bestselling columnist David Brooks. How did the "good enough" essay land on that coveted page? The author won first-place in an essay-writing contest sponsored by the Brooklyn Public Library. This was noted without irony.

Can we really become what we wish? Only you can answer that question for yourself. But that we have been given a song I have no doubt. You cannot express it, and you cannot apply the creative faculties of your mind, however, until you come to terms with what you truly want. Do you know what you want in life? I believe the first chapter, Unwavering Focus, will help you respond meaningfully to that question. It is central to our journey in this book.

I contend that you can take this journey and develop miracles based on how you live moment-by-moment, hour-by-hour, day-by-day. Put another way, based on your habits. The subtitle of this book is, *The Secret of Turning Your Moments Into Miracles*. At the instant that I was standing on a Brooklyn street corner pondering what to use as the subtitle to this book, I saw this sticker on a lamppost:

Call it happenstance, causation, or synchronicity—I'm undecided, but I elected to accept it as a cue, which brings me to another point. For all my talk of success, broadly defined, this is not a secular self-help book. I take a spiritual view of life. When I say spiritual I mean simply extra-physical. I believe that our lives are composed not only of cognition and motor function but that our psyches also possess causative or selective abilities, which surpass ordinary sensory observation. You can use the term New Thought, magick, positive thinking, ESP, or whatever label you like, but I am convinced from personal experience, from generations of testimony, and from the extraordinary questions emergent from fields including neuroplasticity, quantum mechanics, placebo studies, mind-body medicine, and psychical research that our minds interplay with the surrounding world in a manner that displays extra-physical effect on outcome. I have explored that thesis in several books, including *One Simple Idea, The Miracle Club*, and *Magician of the Beautiful*, and I will not fully retread it here. As with those books, I write not as a guru, teacher, or clinician—but only as a seeker. In that vein, my ideas are philosophical and metaphysical.

This book deals with hands-on daily behaviors that in my observation and experience cultivate the extraordinary. We occupy realms that can be considered transcendent, timeless, and spiritual—and at the same time workaday, linear, and habitual. The difference among these is artifice. But we do experience them differently. Likewise, all realms of life and all roles we play within them make varied and valid demands on us. To neglect the so-called spiritual for the material, or vice versa, is a formula for lopsidedness and, ultimately, dissatisfaction. I do not ask you to choose among these worlds. I do not myself. The question of selecting a main approach to life, or choosing one world over another, arose in a 2020 letter from a reader. I quote from it in full since the writer highlighted this issue skillfully:

Hi Mitch,

I'll do my best to be succinct here.

I listened to your two podcasts with Duncan Trussell and I was electrified . . . perhaps literally, ha . . . by the ideas and concepts.

I've since listened to several of your books and those of Neville Goddard, Napoleon Hill, Joseph Murphy and others.*

I've been on some form of spiritual path for many years now, but when I found you and these other great teachers, something profound clicked into place for me.

You have expressed your admiration for Neville Goddard time and time again. I think it wouldn't be out of line to say that you hold him at the top of your esteemed guide/teacher list. As do I.

My most burning question (although I have many) is this: How have you come to reconcile the rather blatant contrasts between Neville and other authors (I'm specifically thinking of Hill) when it comes to the fruition of our desires?

Neville seemed so often to give personal and third party examples of individuals simply thinking

---

* If these names are unfamiliar to you, you'll be learning about them in the chapters ahead.

of a desire (using his methods), only to have that idea manifested. For example: someone thinking/meditating on a house they want, and then receiving it. Or someone wanting a scarf, and then receiving it.

Hill, and you I would say, are more in favor of a method that COMBINES desire with using all available methods of action (meditation, gratitude, love, forgiveness, etc.). This being the most effective and honorable way to achieve one's desires/goals.

I love Neville's way of expressing these ideas so simply and beautifully. I too am able to listen to his teachings over and over again. I'm just really interested in how you've come to reconcile the differences between all of these great teachers.

Again, I am so grateful to have found you and your work.

> Your friend,
> Bryan Nolte
> Green River, Wyoming

I responded this way:

Hi Bryan, That's a perfect framing of the issue, and of my point of view, and I really respect that question. I've wrestled with it myself. I believe that Neville imparts an ultimate truth, which is that intelligence is the final arbiter of reality. But I also believe that in our daily lives there exist many interventions. We experience many laws and forces, and our experience of the world is very "real" within the ordinary sphere of perception. Quantum physics is real, the space between atoms is real—but I nonetheless experience mass when I stub my toe or move an object. So, I feel that the individual must honor what is required in the world of Caesar. Actualization may accompany action in ways that don't require choosing, say, between Neville and a more positivist approach. In any case, we must fulfill the world's expectations—I have to go and buy a ticket, as he did, when going to the theater. Things do arrive through established channels. I hope this helps. Stay in touch.

Best, Mitch

If this book is any kind of adjunct to *The Miracle Club*, and I hope it is, it can be considered a full-bodied exploration of the daily actions that work in concert with the metaphysical. I plan to write a future book focused strictly on the powers of imagination and the ultimate energies of thought, at least as we experience them. But for now my wish is to fulfill a call issued by William James during a symposium at UC Berkeley in 1898 when he urged American philosophers to break with the scholastic traditions of the old world and devise philosophies of "*cash-value*, in terms of particular experience." The emphasis is his, and the phrase forms the title of this chapter. James's call for a philosophy of direct application to life electrified me. I believe that the steps in this book will bring you concrete, measurable benefits in conduct, effectiveness, and experience in the near-term and require only a sincere wish to practice them.

In his 1841 essay "Self-Reliance," Ralph Waldo Emerson wrote that "imitation is suicide." I want to honor that principle, as well. In an era of countless life-coaches minting themselves on YouTube and so on the last thing I want to offer you is fare that could be found elsewhere. Not that I won't say things that others have said, and sometimes better—but I promise you that *everything I write about is something I have lived and that I recommend to you from experience*. There are no platitudes or untested principles in this book. I likewise encourage you to engage the book from your own lived standards: test and verify everything that I say. Throw out what is useless to you. Make these habits and practices your own.

The thirteen "Miracle Habits" are:

HABIT 1: UNWAVERING FOCUS

Holding to one core aim—with absolute passion and singularity—will revolutionize your life. This is life's toughest but most magical bargain. It requires hard decisions and great labor. The payoff is extraordinary.

HABIT 2: TOTAL ENVIRONMENT

Everything is one—including the "inner" and "outer" you. Allow yourself the freedom to radically alter one aspect of life and everything changes. Create a total environment. With no one's rules but your own.

HABIT 3: RADICAL SELF-RESPONSIBILITY

No single habit is more ennobling and charismatic than keeping your word and honoring your commitments—all of them. You must also ask for what you want in return. Value the enacting of solutions over the deciphering of causes.

HABIT 4: SOLIDARITY

I despise cheap paeans to "service." The most unreliable people I know pay lip service to such bromides. Giving and service must be done with muscularity. Identify and act in cases where your help is authentically needed. Help means time, money, and loyalty.

HABIT 5: HONORABLE SPEECH

Gossip, rumor, and frivolous opining do more to degrade you than you can imagine. If you spend just one hour desisting from them you will stand more fully erect.

HABIT 6: GET AWAY FROM CRUEL PEOPLE

Hostile actors, gaslighters, and cruel people abound. They have no place in your life under any circumstances. Burn rotting bridges and watch new ones emerge beneath your feet.

HABIT 7: CHOOSE YOUR COMRADES

Once you've expunged cruelty you must select friends and colleagues who fortify you. Every successful person you witness is an amalgamation of people. Choose your comrades wisely.

HABIT 8: SPEND FOR POWER

Your habits of spending and saving are a core determinant of your power in the world. Spend money only on things that enhance your capacity to produce more of it.

HABIT 9: NEVER DITHER

Acting quickly and with agency is a mark of success. Time dissipates energy. Speed harnesses it. Do not divide your energies or dwell on frivolous projects.

HABIT 10: VITALITY

Strengthening yourself physically is a necessity. If you neglect strength and wellness now it will take all of your energy to correct these deficits later.

HABIT 11: OPPOSITION IS FRIENDSHIP

Failures, setbacks, and even shunning are painful—but they are the only channels of authentic growth. Without them we would remain emotional and intellectual children.

HABIT 12: HARD-WON FAITH

Faith means realizing there are universal principles at your back. Faith can be flexed and strengthened. Make your own rules on the spiritual path.

HABIT 13: RULE IN HELL

You will experience far greater satisfaction by honoring your natural authority rather than conforming in order to win security or prestige. Respectability impedes growth.

I believe these habits will not only improve your life but, in time, will transform it. The first changes may arrive quickly, especially if one of these practices disrupts a negative pattern or shatters a calcified or unproductive behavior. Or the changes may be long term in nature. For most readers, I venture that you will experience immediate—and possibly dramatic—benefits, after which things may plateau. *But if you maintain these habits in a disciplined and steady way you will reach a point where myriad barriers lift and multiple doors open.* You will experience a range of remarkable opportunities.

The reason for sudden change, plateau, and then long-term benefit can be found in the tension of inspiration versus discipline. Discipline matters more than inspiration. Inspiration can hit at propitious moments and make a great difference. But inspiration arrives inconsistently. Discipline, by contrast, is a consistent if less dramatic ensurer of desired, though not always predictable or expected, outcomes. That's why these steps are called habits. They must be constant. The results, when they come, may appear extraordinary. But there exists a rootwork beneath them.

We are taught to view habits in the negative, like smoking, craving caffeine, or engaging in compulsive behavior. Colloquially, we see habits as automatic and incessant. Behavioral scientists do not fully agree on how habits are formed, but brain scans reveal that repeat behaviors forge new neural pathways, which physically reinforce habits. That suggests that significant, positive habits can be cultivated. But behaviorists warn that we can rarely sustain the requisite motivation to form desirable new habits. This book is for people who want to do rare things. If you possess a passionately felt aim, the first and foundational habit of the thirteen in this book, and if you desire it with absolute hunger, that itself will summon the retinue of supporting behaviors. I have watched this occur in others and myself.

I am inspired by something that Napoleon Hill (1883–1970) wrote about the nature of habits. In Hill's 1945 book *The Master Key to Riches*, written eight years after *Think and Grow Rich*, he described what he called "Cosmic Habit Force." I consider it one of the success writer's best insights. Cosmic Habit Force is the cycle of positive repeat behaviors by which nature maintains itself, such as the rotation of the planets, the ebb and flow of tides, and the cycle of seasons. Humans are the only beings that possess the ability to choose their habits, thereby playing a self-selecting role in creation. If you select habits that build your generative forces, you enter into natural, reproductive alignment with laws that enable nature and all of life. This is not dissimilar to concepts found within Taoism and Transcendentalism.

Once you function within this cosmic flow—toward continual growth and expansion—cycles of generativity appear at your back. Hence, you are never truly without resources. With cultivation of the right habits, which means reproductive behaviors and intentions—and barring some equally powerful counter-intervention— you are delivered to the destination you seek like a twig carried downstream in a river. But unlike the twig, the sentient being possesses the possibility of focus, attention, and selection. Choose intelligently—no easy thing—and you enter into this stream.

Hill identifies failure as a necessary course-correction within the scheme of Cosmic Habit Force, a point explored in the chapter on Opposition. Failure is unquestionably painful. But, if allowed to, failure gainfully breaks up stymied, unsuccessful thought patterns, plans, behaviors, and relationships. What replaces them? The actions to which this book is dedicated.

I realize that any self-help book is, by its nature, general. People face myriad challenges at various points in life, which no single text can encompass. As I write these words the nation is facing the early crisis of coronavirus. The applicability of some of what I recommend may be affected by your health; your status as a parent, spouse, or caregiver; your employment or immediate financial needs; and your geography. I am not untouched by diffuse needs and obligations. I am the divorced parent of two adolescent sons, and grew up without parental financial support. For years I worked in corporate publishing, which later on accommodated my work as a writer, but not always.

You may discover the need to reform or alter what I write to fit your current situation. I try, wherever possible, to reflect that consideration. At the same time, I make every step as workable as possible. These habits are radical but more accessible then may first appear. Indeed, part of my wish is to shake up settled thinking about what is possible. I also believe that striving for self-betterment is, in itself, transformative. In that vein, I give the final word of this introduction to poet Ezra Pound from his *Canto 81*: "But to have done instead of not doing/This is not vanity."

HABIT 1

UNWAVERING FOCUS

---

*You cannot get what you want
till you know what you want.*

Few of us know what we want in life. Often we harbor a variety of different aims, some of them in conflict. Such as wanting lots of leisure time while also wishing to excel at work. Sometimes our aims are indirect and unclear, like when we confuse a wish for money with a wish for security. There is clearly overlap between these two goals but they differ. People who suffer the grief of betrayal from a lover sometimes do not know whether they want rapprochement or revenge. The sting of resentment and the glow of lost love coexist in equal measure.

Life is a polarity. Our needs are complex and sometimes paradoxical. There is nothing wrong with a
paradox and nothing that requires "fixing." In many
ways, the capacity to live with paradox is the hallmark
of maturity and wisdom. Yet it is also true—in another
paradox—that to bring something into actuality you
must know and be focused on precisely what you want.
And you must pursue the wished-for condition with
absolute focus and single-minded purpose. Life permits
no halfway measures. So—what do you want? Not just
today, or at this moment, but within the arc of your
existence?

It can seem like an easy question. It is not. It seems
easy only because we grow accustomed to responding
to this question habitually and by rote thought. We
recite homilies in our heads, like "money isn't everything" or "you cannot change other people" or "you
must forgive." I am not challenging the veracity of any
of those statements. But often they do not belong to
you or me. They are social formulas that we accept, just
as blindly as people once accepted their class, family,
or sexual roles. You should accept nothing and seek to
verify everything. Especially when you are determining
what to do with your life.

Once you accept the mantle of self-verification, you
will be able to ask yourself what you want with greater
honesty, passion, and disclosure. And you are asking

privately. You are not submitting your question to a peer group, therapist, or partner. You can, of course, consult with trusted friends or relations. But, in the end, asking what you want from life is a place you must go alone.

This is more than an academic exercise or indulgent self-inquiry. Concentration produces power. This is a natural law. The more densely packed matter (think of a diamond) the harder it grows. The more focused matter (think of photons directed into a laser) the more penetrating it becomes. The same holds true of your psyche. When you select what you want—and you are absolutely truthful and willing to follow your passions—you concentrate your energies with dramatic effectiveness. Outcomes arise that you might never expect. Martial artist Bruce Lee (1940–1973) famously observed about focus and specificity: "I fear not the man who has practiced 10,000 kicks once, but I fear the man who has practiced one kick 10,000 times."

Napoleon Hill called this a Definite Chief Aim, a term he always capitalized and a practice that I continue. Such an aim must be specific and finely focused. There is no room for generality. If you want to become a comic illustrator, police detective, innovative homemaker, political comedian, military officer, or any of the endless permutation of things that a person can be in life—*including those that have no job title or paycheck*—become wholly aware of that.

Our concern, at least at this point, is not money or paying the rent but awareness of and movement toward your aim. A true aim is achievable. It is not a pipe dream or escapism. It is something toward which you can begin gainfully moving almost immediately, even if in small, nascent ways. The measure of authenticity is not whether something can be accomplished but whether actual and pragmatic steps can be taken toward its accomplishment. Otherwise, it's a daydream.

Some readers may wonder why I seem fixated on outer roles of life, particularly career and employment. The fact is, however much you want to define your personhood as something distinct and superseding of work, domestic status, or label, every one of us must be *involved in something*. A teacher of mine told me that one weekend he was laboring to complete the construction of a flight of stairs in a building where a spiritual community he was part of was gathered. My friend was working late into the night on the stairs and couldn't be taken away from the project. A colleague came to him with a blanket and pillow and said sardonically, "You're so identified with those stairs that you should sleep with them." It's a typical (if artfully expressed) rebuke that one hears in various spiritual groups: identification and attachment are an illusory substitute for the true self. But my friend rejected the inference. "He was wrong," he told me. "Because a man has to be involved in something." I consider that an inescapable truth, although I've admittedly interpreted it more broadly than the speaker intended.

Next time someone tells you that you're too identified with something, watch that person closely. Observe how he or she is entangled with intense attachments that he doesn't acknowledge or even recognize, which only deepen the hold of such things. The selection of a Definite Chief Aim is a more transparent and, I believe, positive declaration of dedication and commitment. It meets you where you live: naturally and inevitably involved with the flow of life.

I advise that you do not feel compelled to candy-coat your aim with false paeans to "service," a topic I explore in greater detail later. In attempting to articulate your aim in terms of service—unless you feel that conviction with effortless ease—you are subtly and indirectly endeavoring to "trick" the cosmic scales by using selectively prim language to frame your aim in terms of the benefits it will bring to *others*. At such moments we often use the dictum, "Thy will be done," in an unexamined and self-deceiving way. We do not explore what the Scriptural principle really means—or whether it squares with the metaphysics of lived experience. The fulcrum of unethical behavior is lack of transparency, both within and without us.

I contend that if you are acting with excellence and reciprocity, you are naturally enhancing the common environment. You need not announce it to yourself or others. If philanthropy is authentic to your aim, then pursue that. But don't confuse the issue by seeking to *justify* your aim. Justify it for whom? Being a great schoolteacher is service enough (and it should come with better pay). Being a financier may not sound very romantic in terms of service, but the banking industry has been part of human life since deepest antiquity. Some of the earliest extant documents, like the Dead Sea Scrolls, include commercial contracts. If you demonstrate excellence in your profession—which includes ethical behavior and legal responsibility— you maintain a necessary facet of life. And if you are an activist who wishes to upend conventional systems, and you have good reasons why, that too is expressive of a countervailing and equally necessary force. From where else would arise reform, correction, and potentially newer and better ways of life? Disasters can also arise. So tread carefully.

All that I am really saying is: *Pursue your aim because it is who you are, not because of what is expected of you.* Or what you imagine or have been conditioned to believe is expected. Your aim should be expressive of your nature inasmuch as a cat hunts nocturnally, a bird rides air currents, or a bee gathers pollen—it is the function of your essential self. That is why I am writing these words. Of course, I wish to be read, seen, and paid. And

I take steps to arrange that. But writing this book or delivering a talk is not, strictly speaking, an attachment for me; it is as intrinsic to my selfhood as sleeping at night. If someone does not understand that kind of thing about you, you are in the wrong group, community, or relationship.

If you feel your aim with a sense of absolute passion— if you want it like you want a drink on a hot day—you will find no difficulty dedicating labor to it. Too often we hide behind the question of "how" to do something, which, like claims to want to provide service, often harbor a subtle dishonesty. Notice that when you really want something you do not ask "how." You plan, plot, strategize, and act—but you don't stand as though before a door wondering how to turn the knob. You can see this natural knowingness when people are flirting or attempting to attract a mate. They make eye contact, perform small favors for the person, find excuses to pass by his or her desk at work, display courtesy, attempt humor, find reasons to ask conversational questions, and so on. They effortlessly use their minds and instincts—backed by an unspoken or unrealized sexual attraction—but they do not idly stand there asking "how." They intrinsically know how.

We behave similarly when facing urgency. When students asked spiritual teacher Jiddu Krishnamurti (1895–1986) "how" to behave in the self-determined or nonconformist way that he prescribed, he responded that if you are walking down a road and encounter a cobra, you do not ask *how* to get away; you know full well how. And you do it. Likewise, he told a roomful of young Indian students, when you want to find time to play cricket you do not ask *how*—you steal the time. You sneak away from school, trick your parents or teachers, and find every way to hold that paddle in your hands. When you really want it, you know how.

People used to ask me how, as a former publishing executive and parent of two boys, I found time to write. "I steal time," I told them. Except for my first book *Occult America*, I did not take time away from my kids (and even during *Occult America* I was extensively on the scene); rather I stayed up all night, wrote at my desk at work; wrote during lunch; I watched virtually no movies or TV; I didn't drink; I even took my laptop to a concert and wrote before the performer came out. I would do this kind of thing constantly, and still do.

When you want something badly enough, and without any sense of internal division, you do not ask, you act.

*   *   *

Acting also means working at your necessary tasks repeatedly and constantly. There is no overstating the kind of dedication to which Bruce Lee referred earlier: practicing a single move thousands of times. I am struck by how many people neglect knowing their field or subject. The legendary ad man David Ogilvy (1911–1999) used to say that the single most important element of any advertising campaign is intensity of research. How else would you know what stands out about a product if you haven't immersed yourself in it? Ogilvy's colleague Russ Alben (1929–2012) arrived at the famous slogan for Timex—"Takes a licking and keeps on ticking"— because he delved into customer letters and found that an outsized number of correspondents wrote in to say that their watch had gone through the wash, gotten run over, fallen from a building, got dropped into a paint mixer, got vacuumed up—and kept working. The watch possessed a reputation for ruggedness due to an internal balance mechanism made of a particularly hard alloy. Alben used that knowledge to arrive at one of advertising's most memorable (and truthful) slogans.

Too many "creatives" believe that pithiness arises from out of their clever heads. It does not. It arises from working. I worked in book publishing from 1989 to 2017, starting out as an editorial assistant and becoming a vice-president at Penguin Random House. During that time, I was astonished (and continue to be) at the number of publicists, marketers, and copywriters who literally never read the books they pitch, as if doing so is a dreary bit of trivia. As a result, the book industry produces a great deal of faceless, indistinct marketing material and press releases. Years ago a young publicist came to me with a press release about a book I was publishing by channeler Paul Selig, a longtime friend. Paul has an advanced degree from Yale, has written award-winning plays, and is on the MFA faculty of New York University and Goddard College. This is hardly the usual background for a psychic. Yet none of this appeared in the press release. Instead, the piece was a bland bit of generality about picking your romantic partner or finding the right career. I suggested she read Paul's book and hone in on what is unique about him. The release went out as is. It landed with a thud. Soon after, Paul was positively profiled on *ABC Nightline*—exceedingly rare coverage of a psychic on a network news show. The producers had found him on their own.

A journalism professor of mine once said: "The difference between a good reporter and a mediocre reporter is often one phone call." The effort to check a fact one more time, run a number one more time, review a document one more time is the mark of quality. Curiosity and effort are the dividing line between the good and the merely ordinary. Often people do not want to do extra work. When they do not, it is a mark that they haven't found their true aim. When you're honest with yourself about not wanting to make or return a phone call, or have the ball come to you, it is a sign that you're involved in the wrong activity.

I experienced this myself. It was a very painful but necessary lesson. My first job out of school was as a police reporter at a regional newspaper in northeastern Pennsylvania. One evening, I was chasing a story about a cop accused of rape. I was finding my way around the wall of "blue silence," in which police don't discuss a crime committed by one of their own. That night a city editor pulled me off that story to cover a local Irish festival. I grumbled but trudged off to the festival. Another reporter broke my story. While I was complaining about it in the newsroom the next day, a fellow reporter confronted me and said that I hadn't really wanted the story.

"What?" I asked. "How could you say that?"

"Look," she said, "I know you were pissed off when you got sent you to cover the Irish festival. But you should've refused. You should've said no. You didn't really want the cop story badly enough. You let it get taken from you."

I was flattened by the truth of what she said. I was sick inside—because I knew she was right. I vowed that night to either recommit to journalism or get out of it. I would not hang around my field as a mediocrity. I got out. It was one of the most important decisions of my life, and it ultimately led me to rediscover myself as a writer. But focused on subjects that are truer to who I am.

Finding your purpose doesn't necessarily mean scaling some great career height, but demonstrating honesty with yourself. Wherever it leads. I have a close friend who didn't find his way in life until he realized that he wanted a more private and leisurely life than he did a highly public or hard-driving career. His decision not only helped him but also his adolescent daughters, and it's worth exploring.

My friend graduated as valedictorian of his Long Island high school and majored in physics in college, where we roomed together. (We had actually met earlier at the beta launch of a fantasy roleplaying game called *Villains and Vigilantes*. So there you have it.) After college, he entered an Ivy League doctoral program in physics. Within a few months, however, he discovered that it wasn't what he wanted to do with his life. He left the graduate program and bopped around for a few months in retail jobs. He felt stung by the lack of money. He decided he was going to attend law school and get a corporate law job so that he would never have to stress about money again. He got a perfect score on the LSAT—"he's like death," a mutual friend remarked—

and entered law programs at New York University and Princeton. But after graduating and landing his coveted corporate law job, he once more felt nonplussed. Corporate law wasn't what he wanted, either.

He was interested in foreign affairs and particularly in international trade agreements. So he found a job with one of the government's trade commissions, negotiating and settling trade disputes, which necessitated moving to Washington, D.C. The job didn't pay anywhere near what he could've earned in a corporate job. But it afforded him something that kind of job never would: leisure time. When you're a corporate lawyer you live and die by billable hours. Corporate lawyers easily work 60 hours a week or more. It's grueling. But it's the only track to partnership. My friend worked hard, but not like that. Nor was he paid like it. But he made a startling and admirable admission to me: "I discovered that I really value my leisure time."

He liked sci-fi novels, roleplaying games (yes, again), Renaissance fairs, and movies. He was self-honest about this and desired work that permitted this aspect of his personality. It helped the people who he loved, too. A divorce left him as the residential parent of two adolescent daughters. He was able to successfully raise them, and to be on the scene for them as a parent, precisely because he didn't have an all-consuming corporate law job. One well-selected aim can cover a lot of different bases. My friend's wish to maintain his free time also made him an effective single father when circumstances required it. Eventually he remarried to a vibrant woman who shared all of his interests. The symmetry—one could even say miracle—of gelling his whole life together arose from the honesty and admission of wanting a job that also afforded him a life. I've always deeply respected him for it. He is powerful because he realized that his aim was chiefly about *how* he wanted to live.

Now, in writing this passage I am keenly aware that my friend, as a person of uncommon ability and circumstance, was able to exercise choices in life that are not open to all of us. There are other factors involved too, such as geography, background, and getting certain breaks. Lots of people want to spend more time with their kids but cannot. The demand for health insurance alone (something I cover later) places a terrible burden on working parents. But the point I wish to bring out is that my friend's honesty about what he wanted delivered him to a lifestyle that benefited himself and others—and provided distinct relief when domestic circumstances doubled his load as a parent. This is why I contend that one sincere aim can cover many needs.

*   *   *

Once you have a sense of your aim, I believe strongly that you should write it down. Not on a device but with a pencil and paper. Your aim should be something that you can boil down to a simple sentence. If that presents difficulty it probably tells you something about the clarity of your goal.

If index cards didn't exist I'd have to invent them. I believe that you should be able to make a totem of your aim and carry it with you on a card that you readily consult. (Use clear packing tape to laminate your card.) This not only creates a reminder, but I believe that the act of making a physical declaration amounts to actualizing something in the world, however small at first. I do not regard such things as trite. Some of the most effective and impressive people I have known—artists, athletes, novelists—have made a written declaration of an aim. It creates a subtle pull on the psyche.

Earlier in my career I learned a lesson about the importance of writing things down. Once upon a time, I was an editor of political books, which can make my later work as a historian and publisher of alternative spirituality seem discursive. But twists and curves are the natural contours of any path. As a young editor I published Colonel Harry G. Summers (1932–1999), a Vietnam officer whose book *On Strategy* is considered perhaps the greatest analysis of the U.S. failure in Vietnam. Summers argued that the Army was capable of defeating the Viet Cong. None of the opposing circumstances were insurmountable and, in fact, American forces almost always prevailed on the battlefield.

So what, from a military perspective, went wrong? Summers argued that the nation's political leadership never attempted to build a "moral consensus" for the war. President Lyndon Johnson never asked Congress for a formal declaration of war, which many policymakers saw as an outdated formality. Hence, without a formal declaration, and the political process underscoring it, the public never really supported the conflict. Policymakers lacked the consent and mandate to authorize an overwhelming effort, relying instead on Defense Secretary Robert McNamara's chimerical (and failed) notion of a "limited war." The result was quagmire, carnage, and moral confusion.

Without a mandate, policymakers tied their own hands. Year after year, America's political leadership authorized the Army to muddle along in a half-in and half-out effort, which eroded opinion at home and frustrated commanders. As Summers wrote, the missing ingredient—the lost grail of victory—was the failure to secure public trust. Without popular consent, backed by formal declaration, the war should never have been fought. No nation, he wrote, should commit to conflict without determination for swift victory and restoration of peace. President George W. Bush and his circle of neoconservative policy advisors—whom Summers derisively called the "whiz kids"—inflicted this problem anew on the nation in the Iraq War, which was waged with murky justification and limited public commitment.

All endeavors, of whatever nature, follow one key rule, to which I've been alluding. You must be "all in." You must select a goal to which you can dedicate yourself with unreserved commitment—or don't do it at all. When you decide on a goal, "burn the fleet"—throw yourself into it with total dedication and leave no way out. Change your aim only when necessitated by new evidence or unforeseen circumstance. And even then do so only after great consideration. As I explore in the section on Comrades, sometimes the perception of failure arises from your having partnered with the wrong people. That can be fixed. Other times, as we'll explore in the section on Opposition, failure itself provides vital corrections. In any case, once your declaration is made, it is vital never to underestimate the dignity and power that arise from persistence. These traits, more than anything else, salve personal failure and eventually replace it with renewal.

Society conspires to rob you of your aim and focus. Appeals for your consumer dollars are relentless. Social media is built on distraction and bickering. Peers often tell you to take it easy, to be well rounded, not to work so hard. But excellence does not take it easy. Nor are you obligated to be versed in whatever is popular in media unless it forwards your aim. Indeed, I believe that what we colloquially call "well rounded" or easygoing often means a dispersal of energies and focus. "You're not hungry when you're dead," as a friend puts it. Someone easygoing did not engineer or program the device you may be viewing or listening to this book on.

As you hone your aim, you may find that friends and coworkers are always trying to get you to watch movies, sports events, or participate in media that may interest them but not you. Honor your relationships—but also honor your instincts. We can absorb and retain only so much information. What appeals to you in media, as in company (something explored in the section on Comrades), usually has to do with expanding your sense of power. This cannot occur if you feel bound to other people's ideas of what you ought to be imbibing. Magician Anton LaVey (1930–1997), a stirring and unique intellect, put it this way in his 1986 essay "Don't Recycle Your Brain":

> I refuse to partake of trendy or pop input. Not so much because it usually replaces valued old information, but because it will "mediocritize" me. It will

dilute my special kind of knowledge bank (which has allowed me to remain unique) to a sort of common knowledge catchall. It will render me more adaptable to the common denominators of the herd, but much less adaptive as a role model to others. Rather than being possessed of data that gives me social distinction, I will be able to discuss the same movies, plays, singers, TV shows and stars, current events, sports, etc., as everyone else. Thus, I won't *look* like everyone else, but the moment I open my mouth, I'll *sound* like them.

Anton's principle was that all new data should be "augmentive" of whatever valued ideas, concepts, and techniques you already possess. This does not mean that you shouldn't experience something wholly new; even such a break provides a fresh perspective from which to measure your own ideas and thought forms. The point is that you don't just *giveaway* your attention to whatever comes along, or whatever peer activity you're directed toward. For example, I virtually never watch videos people send me. It would prove an unmanageable time suck. When I select novels or media, even for entertainment, it is usually something that augments my sense of aim, style, personhood, and my effort to craft a "total environment," another concept of Anton's, which I explore in the following chapter.

A friend once teased me: "Mitch doesn't care whether a work of art is good so long as it fits his *Weltanschauung*" (a slightly disreputable German term for worldview). To that, I plead guilty. I sympathize with certain under-realized books or movies because they circle around an idea that I like, such as the 2011 dark comedy *Wuss* about a bullied high school teacher who makes a morally ambiguous (and deadly) choice. My intake is actually very broad but often augmentative of concepts that I am working with. Otherwise, I would be unfocused and overwhelmed.

While I was writing this book a few people on social media asked how I was able to write so much. One even inquired whether I use ghostwriters. (NEVER I replied in one of my few violations of a personal rule against using all caps.) One of the ingredients that feeds my output is the principle I have just described: never deplete your time (even your leisure time) through frivolity, but always look to build upon theses, ideas, and insights that are vital to you. That provides more raw material and connective tissue between seemingly diffuse topics than you might imagine.

Many people identify procrastination as their greatest barrier. In a certain sense the term procrastination is a euphemism. Procrastination and fear are the same.

The best way to approach procrastination is to first acknowledge it as fear. Once you've made that step, it is less important to ask yourself *why* you're afraid (which can prompt an endless cycle of self-reflection, producing another form of procrastination) than it is to apply yourself to the task at hand. If you cannot do this, you must ask yourself whether you really *want* the thing that you're going after or if you're willing to sacrifice success, relationships, or remuneration—whatever may be at stake—to appease your fear.

This is why it's essential to choose a Definite Chief Aim for which you feel passion. During periods of dejection, failure, fear of failure, or setback—and these will come, surely as every cycle of nature—the emotional intensity of your aim will push you forward.

We cannot talk ourselves out of fear. To do so requires pitting thought against emotion. But emotion is stronger than thought. Pitting thought against emotion is like pitting steam power against nuclear power—the latter wins every time. But we can pit emotion against emotion. The passion that you feel for your aim can outweigh fear of failure, provided you've chosen rightly. "All depends on really wanting," C.S. Lewis wrote in *Mere Christianity*.

Personal excellence also helps overcome fear. A good friend is actor Yul Vazquez who you would recognize from many screen performances including his role in the 2020 HBO miniseries *The Outsider*. Yul points out that every audition is hit or miss—the performer may or may not be right for the part. But what is vitally important, and what helps the artist stand on his feet time after time, is accurate knowledge of his own abilities. Yul puts it this way:

> It's not up to anybody else to determine if someone is good at what they do. The person reaches a certain point—for the artist it doesn't come early, it comes later—where they realize that they are good at what they do; and they may or may not be right for a part but the verdict of whether they are good is already in.

Your earned sense of personal excellence protects you. If you can reach that point, whatever the nature of your work, you have gone a long way toward overcoming the debilitating effects of fear.

In 1937, Napoleon Hill wrote about the destructiveness of fear—and of how fear itself detracts more from your quality of life than nearly anything that could actually befall you. "Kill the habit of worry," Hill wrote, "in all its forms, by reaching a general, blanket decision that nothing which life has to offer is worth the price of worry." Remember those words. They capture one of the key principles of effective living. If you capitulate to fear you have declared it your highest value.

HABIT 2

TOTAL ENVIRONMENT

Don't settle for someone else's world.

Nothing is more dulling of possibility than conformity. Not that any of us are ever free of the pull of peer pressure. But we capitulate far too easily, and with too little thought. This is true not only in terms of appearance, but also in matters of transportation, education, problem solving, family structure, sexuality, media, politics, and even in issues of life and death. Within seemingly confining circumstances, we overlook or prejudicially reject broad latitudes for action.

In terms of your sense of self, it is easy to underestimate the power of dress, adornment, body art, gait, tone, style, and name. These things have a tremendous and holistic impact on the nature of your experience and your effect on others. I know people who have changed or altered their names to suit a desired persona, and I celebrate the practice. But owning your birth name in a wholly independent and self-selected way can be equally powerful. Seen on one level, The Beatles is a goofy name for a rock band. Yet what name better summons the energy and creativity of the sixties? They remade it from a made-up word into a magical one.

I once wished that I had changed my name, since Mitch Horowitz can sound like your orthodontist. But, as with the Beatles, I realized that a name assumes a whole different tenor based on what is associated with. Here are some names that might not sound very romantic, but they summon incredible cultural meaning: Marvin Gaye; Allen Ginsberg; Norman Mailer; Naomi Campbell; Manolo Blahnik. Maybe Ralph Lifshitz never could have become America's premier designer without the last name Lauren, but the odds are in favor of your being able to transform your name's associations. If you're at a time in your career when changing your name is no longer an option, do not fret—vow to occupy your name in such a way that makes it a power term. Apropos of that, I advise against changing your name or byline late in your career. Done too late it seems fickle. The Edge had to become The Edge at seventeen, or not at all.

*   *   *

In the same vein as changing a name, I also support cosmetic surgery *if that's your considered personal choice.* The point is not adhering to some perpetually moving target of youth or perfection but facilitating a sense of personal comfort and ease. That alone, and not pleasing another person, is the point of cosmetic surgery. It is wholly individualized. There is no one-size-fits-all psychological solution to appearance or self-acceptance, and it insults the self-determinism of the individual to suggest as much. The key is doing what allows you to own a sense of self.

Self-acceptance can take varying forms. I have seen balding fashion models appear in *Hommes Magazine*, including on the cover. They look incredible. Whatever look or trait you *own* is what makes you magnetic. Nothing else. On one hand, you should not permit yourself to be pressured into cosmetic procedures; but if that is your choice, then do not get lost in Hamlet-like handwringing over whether you're capitulating to "societal standards." Every society, from the Ancient Egyptians to the Native Siberians, had keenly felt standards of beauty. The ancient Greeks idealized the chiseled male body. The Maya, for reasons difficult for modern people to fathom, valued cross-eyes. Cultural standards of beauty are a facet of living in any community. You can abide by them, you can resist them, or you can create something new. The key is whatever allows you to own your sense of self. That never requires apology.

I believe that dressing how you like is profoundly important. I wear t-shirts, leather boots and jackets, and have lots of tattoos. One night I went to a KISS concert in Brooklyn and painted my nails. I've never stopped. It makes me feel happy and at home. Do not underestimate the power intrinsic in this. Life is not "inner" and "outer"—it is whole. And you will be able to verify this when you discover what a change in comportment and appearance can mean. This is not always true, of course, but it is often enough to be treated as a general rule.

There is something to be said for being a dramatist, whatever your aims in life. Marketing executive Jane Evans told a wonderful story at the website Refinery29 of reversing career anemia and combatting ageism by reverting her hair to its natural white and chopping it into a spiky punk pixie-cut:

I started my career in advertising when I was just 20 and was headhunted out to Australia at 25, where I worked with big name brands like Revlon and Maserati. I decided to come back to the UK in 2013 [at age 50] after receiving a call for more female leaders in the advertising industry, so I applied, but I found myself continually ignored. I remember people saying so many ageist things to my face. For example, I'd go for a job but the employer would tell me: "I'd give you one but you'd end up as the old lady at the back of the department doing the shit no one else wants."

In the three years that followed, I felt like I was becoming more and more invisible, so I started working with much smaller clients just to keep a roof over my head. Then, one evening at work drinks, I was subjected to a shocking tirade of sexist, ageist verbal abuse by a client of mine. It felt like the deepest, darkest patriarchy was spewing out of him. After the tirade, and being taken off a major part of the project, I found out all the women were paid £100 a day less so I walked and escaped to Paris on a whim.

The idea to overhaul my image and chop off all my long, dark hair hit me when I was sitting outside a café in the city centre, people watching. The women I kept seeing walking by all had their own individual style and they all totally owned their age, including their natural hair colour. No one was trying to be younger and they just looked so cool being themselves. As soon as I got back to London, it was like a lightbulb moment, a switch flicking. I walked into a salon and said to the hairdresser: "No more old lady, give me old punk!" I told her to take all my cascading hair off and to give me my natural hair colour, which is white.

At this age, you only have one chance to completely reinvent yourself because your hair changes, your skin changes, your shape changes and so on. It's a great time to think, Who am I? What do I look like? What do I do? I felt like I was released from so much after I cut my hair, particularly in business. Interestingly, I'm no longer sexually objectified. When I had longer hair (and I don't really have any evidence to back this up), I got the feeling that I could be taken advantage of because I was trying to look younger and this seemed to encourage the ageism that I faced. My ex-client shocked me so much that evening before I quit, but it spurred me to realise that I wasn't the only woman who was facing things like this. It made me look ageism in the face, which has been incredible. I'm going over the other side of menopause and nobody tells you how powerful and empowering it is. Add on top of that a whole new look and it's more than just changing your appearance.

Evans made this testimony at age fifty-six and her photos support her words—she exudes confidence and formidability.

* * *

As a friend puts it, "You should be able to be made into an action figure—and be immediately recognizable." This doesn't mean presenting yourself in a histrionic manner. But rather having a trademark look, daily uniform, or distinctive *something*. Dress is very important. A martial uniform, for example, commands respect—notice how you treat police officers, soldiers, or firemen. A casual-dressing novelist I know once made several visits to a friend in the hospital. One time as an experiment he went in a business suit rather than his usual street clothes. The staff treated him much more respectfully. He never forgot it.

Virtually every notable figure in recent history, whether politician, playwright, artist or activist, had a certain physical characteristic or gesture that you can immediately identify. For Franklin Roosevelt it was his extended cigarette holder. For Oscar Wilde his flowing cape. For commentator George Will his bowties. For Elvis his pompadour and sneer. For Fran Lebowitz her laconic, can-I-go-home-now? expression. When formulating their image in the early 1970s, the members of KISS vowed never to appear in public without their makeup. In a sense, that's true of all these figures.

In early 2020, *The New York Times* profiled model and fashion designer Olivia Palermo—the article contained an offhand observation that I thought warranted a closer look:

> You will never see her at home on a Sunday in sweats and a greasy ponytail. She probably does not do this off-camera either: Ms. Palermo wrote in a Q. and A. on the website of her trainer, Tracy Anderson, that "Sunday is not an excuse for looking badly dressed."

I am aware of how ridiculous and pie-in-the-sky that can sound to working parents. But sit with it for a moment. Palermo isn't saying that the individual must pursue some impossible standard of glamour. (Of course, she *does* trade in that as a fantasy, which is nothing new. Look at humanity's ancient myths of great warriors and princesses.) Rather Palermo is saying that your sense of self, your look, your composure should always be present. That doesn't mean coiffing yourself at every private moment. But when you're in public or hauling your kids somewhere, you can look neat and put together. That not only aids your sense of self but keeps you from getting swallowed up in a single role, such as that of parent, employee, caregiver, and so on. It helps you remain yourself. And if you're an artist, performer, or someone intent on cultivating an image, it is important to project that image consistently. I don't mean that in a vain way. Remember: we are interested in dissolving the artifice of inner and outer. *It's all one thing.* Who you are is a whole. Inasmuch as any form of self-expression requires discipline, so does the so-called outer. People in fashion understand a lot about human nature; do not be among the eye-rollers who feel they have nothing to learn from them.

One day I watched myself on television wearing my then-usual blazer and I thought: that doesn't look like me. I generally wear t-shirts. I decided to start doing that on television. Producers for documentary series usually send out dress guidelines before shoots. Men are told to dress in "business casual," to avoid black, or sometimes to dress as though they are going on a job interview. I decided to ignore all of this (and even to avoid the awkward conversation that I was ignoring it). The only concession I would make was to turn my shirt inside out if asked to obscure a licensed band logo. I felt vastly more at ease when dressed this way. I was warned that showing up in t-shirts and tattoos would close doors for me. The opposite occurred. Instead of just being another talking head, I was an individual. It didn't come automatically and it didn't come overnight. For years I stymied my sense of self by a desire to please authority. But in pleasing others you become forgettable.

I am not suggesting that you force an affect. To adopt traits you don't possess is a surefire way to play the fool. For example, I am not sardonic. To attempt to be sardonic would make me wobbly on my feet and insincere. Cool means self-assured and detached from jockeying for praise. You cannot wear someone else's shoes and be magnetic. I know an earnest person who damaged his career and reputation because he made the kinds of wisecracks that he thought it was the job of an intellectual to do. People resented him. He came off as insecure and hostile.

At the same time, I'm not saying to "act natural," which is one of those meaningless expressions. Society, media, peers, and family load us down with so many preconceptions that it can require a lifetime to rediscover the self you left behind at age three or four. Hence, we do not always *know* how to act natural. But if you give yourself time, and you begin to act in favor of small wishes (for example, a preference for boots over sneakers) you will begin to glean hints of your innate proclivities.

A brilliant spiritual teacher and social critic named A.R. Orage (1873–1934) used to tell people to take careful note of their preferences, including in basic matters like food, bathing and grooming habits, desired times of sleep and rising, speaking or remaining silent. You may not always be able to act upon your preferences, he said, but you ought to at least know what they are.

A small number of people are graced with the kind of fluidity of movement and natural beauty that makes them at ease and magnetic in nearly any situation. But I am also struck by the numbers of people in cities like Paris, New York, and Los Angeles who do not possess these natural gifts but instead have the aesthetic sensibilities to magnetize themselves; they have a sense of personal theatricality—not as an affect but as an expression of the persona they wish to embody. I have gazed into the faces and at the physical forms of people who, possessed of a lesser sense of self, might appear ordinary, but instead they are striking because of the ability to craft themselves into the beings that they really are. True style does not obfuscate, it reveals.

The person to whom this book is dedicated says: "Everything tells a story." What story do you want to tell about yourself?

In the vein of telling your story, it must be acknowledged that almost all of us are engaged to some greater or lesser degree in marketing ourselves and our points of view. Given that reality, I recommend that you get to know the work of a man toward whom I harbor deeply mixed feelings, but grudging respect: Edward Bernays (1819–1995). A nephew to Sigmund Freud and an imperious figure once known as the "father of public relations," Bernays was a master at manufacturing media and personal narratives. Although he died nearly a quarter-century ago, his fingerprints remain etched on many facets of modern life.

Bernays' 1923 book *Crystalizing Public Opinion* captures uncomfortable truths about the malleability of public opinion and perception. What are fame and influence but perception? Bernays grasped this insight early in his career. In striving to influence perception, Bernays understood the power of disruption. Five years before his death, the PR master told historian Stuart Ewen: "A good public relations man advises his client . . . to carry out an overt act . . . interrupting the continuity of life in some way to bring about a response."

This could be understood as manufacturing a news event—like funding and unveiling a research study. Or candidate Donald Trump descending the escalator at his eponymous tower in New York City to denounce undocumented immigrants. Or a generation earlier Yippies and activists vowing to levitate the Pentagon in protest of the Vietnam War. Or rock icons The Who smashing their instruments on stage in a pre-punk display of adolescent rage.

When I was a kid an urban legend made the rounds that the Sex Pistols had pissed on the Statue of Liberty. This never happened. But the rumor alone served the purpose of building a sense of riotous anarchy around the group's image. During the Pistols' short-lived 1978 U.S. tour, manager Malcolm McLaren booked them chiefly into Bible-Belt venues. Why? To profit from the outrage the band was sure to generate in more socially conservative parts of the country.

Bernays said that the provocateur and the public are locked in symbiosis, and that the politician, influencer, or message-maker had to fill an authentically felt need on the part of his audience. (This also suggests the degree to which opposing sides are related—they feed on each other.) "Public opinion," Bernays wrote in *Crystalizing Public Opinion*, "is the resultant of the interaction between two forces"—opinion-shaper and needful public. You must fill a perceived and emotionally charged need, such as for beauty, defeat of an enemy, or promotion of health. The list is endless but it must be keenly felt.

In deciphering the public mood, Bernays insisted that the artist, policymaker, influencer, fashion or ad designer must remember that the public consists of "generalists." They depend upon easily accessed and trusted sources. Trusted sources are able to read the community's moods and brandish credentials to which community members relate. Bernays believed that communities are almost always polarized or in opposition to each other. How do you change minds in such a polarized climate? Bernays wrote: "It is seldom effective to call names or attempt to discredit the beliefs themselves." Rather, the influencer, "after examination of the sources of established beliefs, must either discredit the old authorities or create new authorities" by fomenting "mass opinion against the old belief or in favor of the new."

Roger Ailes (1940–2017), the Svengali of Fox News, mastered the concept of how to "discredit the old authorities." His insight gave rise to Fox's "Fair and Balanced" slogan as a response to perceived liberal bias in the media. But it must be noted that you cannot just mint a slogan and you're off and running as a new, upstart authority. Bernays observed that public mood, opinion, and outlook keenly matter—and must be studied or instinctively sensed.

As Bernays further grasped, people are motivated by self-gain. Few of us acknowledge this, but it informs most of our political, cultural, and consumer choices.

Ailes understood that millions of Americans believed that their personal experience was not being adequately reflected in the "mainstream" media. Whether, or on what terms, one wants to support or dispute that notion, Ailes' insight proved sufficiently correct so that his approach attained Bernays' sought-after symbiosis.

I'd venture that most people reach their political views based on what makes them feel safe. Gun ownership versus gun control is a prima-facie case. Yet such perspectives are not set in concrete. "The instinct of self-preservation," Bernays wrote, "one of the most basic of human instincts, is most flexible." In questions of safety, new or unseen facts matter. If those facts can reach people.

What's more, people care about how a position, opinion, or vote makes them look to others. "Man is never so much at home as when he is on the bandwagon," Bernays wrote. The larger point, as he saw it, is that: "No idea or opinion is an isolated factor. It is surrounded and influenced by precedent, authority, habit, and all other human motivations." In other words, people judge a cause by the company it places them in. Hence, PETA and other animal-rights groups have been very canny to use models and celebrities as spokespersons. That is sometimes called the "key people" strategy, a term coined by early twentieth-century evangelist Frank Buchman, whereby you enlist a spokesperson or charter member who exudes success and with whom others want to be associated.

Bernays also wrote that crowds love a contest. This crowd/contest dynamic fuels the sarcastic political bickering that populates Twitter. The sense of contest taps into what Bernays called "the 'herd' point of view," and it results in mass audiences, mass products, and mass-media events. What's more, the individual, for better or worse (and usually worse), is most heedful of voices that he or she identifies as part of the same "buffalo herd."

Kanye West reads Bernays, particularly his 1928 book *Propaganda*. I learned this from a well-placed colleague who said that the artist, following several rejections, sold his apparel line to Adidas based not on comfort or versatility, but on the brand's image of exclusivity and knowingness. "A thing may be desired not for its intrinsic worth or usefulness," Bernays wrote in *Propaganda*, "but because he [the consumer] has unconsciously come to see in it a symbol of something else, the desire for which he is ashamed to admit to himself." In other words, we buy for image or prestige.

Having reviewed the master's principles, I am thrown onto the question: Is there any ethical application of Bernays' thought? I believe there are at least morally neutral applications of Bernaysism. I have no necessary argument with the disruptive spectacle created by fashion designers, hip-hop artists, filmmakers, or metal bands. It can also be argued that there are ethical applications of Bernaysism based simply on who is wielding the scalpel. A trademark slogan, article of clothing, or maxim are not, of themselves, bad things. Think: "Yes We Can" (Obama); "Happy Days Are Here Again" (Roosevelt), "Come Home, America" (George McGovern), or "And Now—Win the Peace" (Labour Party).

In large measure, the ethical application of Bernays' insights rests, finally, on what one is *unwilling* to use.

Anger, hostility, perpetual contest, and public division have severely strained our culture. Personally, I would not use such things to sell products or to sell myself. Another great manipulator—who I venture was more principled than Bernays—made this observation: "I do not believe that divisions purposely caused can ever lead to good." That was Niccolò Machiavelli, writing in 1532 in *The Prince*.

If anger is required to sell something, I do not want a piece of it. But if I, as an author, can use Bernays' ideas to build an audience for a message that extolls, let's say, the value of a broadly defined spiritual search, then I see such methods as fair game. I believe some variant of this is true for every communicator.

We settle too quickly for conventional choices, like owning a car. Or owning a bed. A bed epitomizes convention, at least if you don't want one. I personally throw two thin futons on the floor. I can roll them up and stash them if I like. I don't want to dedicate a whole room to a bed. When I host out-of-town friends I roll out a thin Thai futon for them. You may or may not want to stay at my place—but it is inexpensive, space saving, and comfortable, if in a slightly Spartan way.

Now, depending upon where you live, a car is vitally necessary for employment, shopping, and so on. One of

New Thought's finest intellects, David Spangler, used car ownership to illustrate an important point, which is worth exploring on its own. In his book *Everyday Miracles*, Spangler made the observation that when working with people who wanted to manifest (I would say select*) something into their lives it usually became clear that they were seeking "not an object but a condition." Spangler noted that whatever you bring into your life is holistic: "*When you manifest, you are manifesting a new identity, a new you.*" He calls it co-incarnational or Gaian Manifestation.

In that vein, Spangler described the experience of working with a friend who was trying to manifest a car. "But in fact," Spangler wrote in *The Laws of Manifestation*, "I'm not only manifesting a car:

> I'm also manifesting a relationship to the petroleum industry that supplies the gas I'll use; a relationship to the government that issues licenses and to insurance companies that sell me insurance; a relationship to the infrastructure of transportation, such as roads, and the need for taxes to maintain that infrastructure; a relationship to the service industry that will help me maintain my car, such as mechanics, and garages and tire compa-

---

* I explain my reasons in *The Miracle Club*.

nies. I also need to find a place to park and house my car.

As Spangler and his friend worked together, they began to see the web of connections—desirable or not— required to sustain this piece of technology. After a guided meditation the friend told him:

"I really don't want a car. I don't support the gasoline industry, I don't like the paving over of the country-side to make roads and parking lots, I don't want to give insurance companies my money. That's why I can't manifest a car. I don't want to manifest every-thing that comes with it." I then helped him see that what he really wanted to manifest was transporta-tion, which could take different forms. What form might best suit him? "A bicycle," he said. "I really want to manifest a bicycle." The next day he got a phone call from a friend who was leaving town. "I can't take my bike with me," his friend said. "Would you like to have it?" Within twenty-four hours to realizing what he really wanted to manifest, he had the transportation he needed.

This passage is not really about a car but about flexible thinking. I like Spangler's example so much that I am seizing upon both the principle and its object. We settle too quickly for what we think we need, whether a car or something else, and hence neglect how we want to live—what environment we want to create around ourselves. I bike nearly everywhere in New York City. If you meet me chances are I'll be carrying a biking helmet (it has saved my life and I won't bike without it) and strap-on bike lights for nighttime riding, which I keep in my backpack. For me, urban biking gives access to a whole environment: riding is healthier (if not always safer, hence my gear); it is fast; it is cheap; and I enjoy the biking culture. When I was a kid I used to ride on a school bus. I hated it. It was like a rolling version of *Lord of the Flies*. If I had to do it over I would bike everywhere, including in rain and snow. Clothes dry. Biking today gives me a feeling of independence.

I believe we are in time of great flux in terms of education, especially with the crisis in student debt, and I would carefully consider where to dedicate your education dollars and years, or those of a child. Some of the most inspiring and successful people I know did not attend college. They went directly into their careers, including gunsmithing, fashion design, tech, and film directing. I believe the trades are a wonderful career, including plumbing, contracting, landscaping, and hairstyling. I often tell my two sons, "You can be an electrician who loves opera, can't you?" My only college courses of value were mathematics and a few composition and journalism classes. (I grew up with the absurd notion that I wasn't "good at math." In college I went from getting an "incomplete" in proficiency math to an A+—because I had help from a roommate who was actually capable of teaching math.) Those were probably the only classes that imparted what I consider a lasting education. Otherwise, I learned my craft as a writer at the student newspaper, where I worked long hours.

I urge parents and kids to think flexibly about higher education. The costs are stratospheric and the payoff is questionable unless one is entering the professions, sciences, or receiving some kind of certification, like physical therapy. (In that vein, I am a big fan of community colleges.) In fairness, I was an English major so maybe I am closing the door after the fact. But I do believe that greater educative purpose is served by reading the classics (for which you'll rarely find time in working life) and in honing your writing skills rather than engaging in deconstructive theory (spoon please). Lest that sound kneejerk, I have witnessed waves of young graduates with fancy humanities degrees stream into publishing often with boundless opinions but with scant and feckless work habits. I believe that discipline and rigor give a person the foundation for experiment and growth. Experiment as an end to itself leads to idolizing experiment as a way to excuse absence of training.

At one point in my publishing career I thought about taking business classes or enrolling in a continuing education program to get an MBA. Thankfully, I was dissuaded by educator and author Ronald Gross, who is responsible for popularizing the term "lifelong learning." Ron convinced me that I could learn just as much on the job by throwing myself into the financial details of my work and collaborating with business managers, which would prove both educative and career advancing, and also save a lot of money. Ron was correct on every count.

One of the signature pleasures of my career was working with filmmaker David Lynch on his book *Catching the Big Fish*, in which he talked about art, inspiration, and Transcendental Meditation. One of David's key points is the need to surround yourself with a workshop environment. And to have time to immerse yourself in your work. When inspiration or ideas hit, they must be acted on or they will fade. Hence, the painter, the illustrator, the musician must have his or her tools readily in reach, and must also have the time to act. I realize too well how difficult if not impossible that kind of environment is for many people. Many of us have children or work schedules or domestic arrangements that preclude that kind of setup. It is not always possible. But it is an ideal toward which to strive.

As a writer, I get ideas in the middle of the night. Sometimes I cannot get up and work on these things, but I will create a mnemonic device to preserve an idea until my waking hours. I created such a device the night before writing these words. I devised a sentence in my head: *Henri can and will not complain.* What does it mean? It encapsulates three ideas that occurred to me in the moments between sleep and wakefulness (a highly supple mental period called hypnagogia): 1) I wanted to cite David's principle about environment and the book that got him on the idea, *The Art Spirit* by Robert Henri. 2) I wanted to add a section about the payoff of seemingly "impossible" hard work based on a colleague once telling me "you can, and you will" when I complained of being unable to handle something. And, finally, 3) I wanted to add a segment about the importance of avoiding frivolous complaints. Hence: *Henri can and will not complain.* You'll find each of these segments in the book. You're reading the first one right now.

Mnemonic devices, such as a mental picture, symbol, or sentence, are not the equivalent of working on what you want when inspiration strikes. But they are the closest non-physical adjunct to having your workshop ready, and they are a means of preserving an idea.

As mentioned, I carry my laptop with me almost everywhere—literally. I have had it with me at concerts. My intention is to be able to write at any time, at any moment.

I want to quote the passage that I referenced from David's book, where he also makes an important point about the nature of a Definite Chief Aim:

In high school I read Robert Henri's book *The Art Spirit*, which prompted the idea of the art life. For me, living the art life meant a dedication to painting—a complete dedication to it, making everything secondary.

That, I thought, is the only way you're going to get in deep and discover things. So anything that detracts from that path of discovery is not part of the art life, in that way of thinking. Really the art life means a freedom. And it seems, I think, a hair selfish. But it doesn't have to be selfish; it just means that you need time.

Bushnell Keeler, the father of my friend Toby, always had this expression: "If you want to get one hour of good painting, you have to have four hours of uninterrupted time."

And that's basically true. You don't just start painting. You have to sit for a while and get some kind of mental idea in order to go and make the right moves. And you need a whole bunch of materials at the ready. For example, you need to build framework stretchers for the canvas. It can take a long time just to prepare something to paint on. And then you go to work. The idea just needs to be enough to get you started, because, for me, whatever follows is a process of action and reaction. It's always a process of building and then destroying. And then, out of this destruction, discovering a thing and building on it. Nature plays a huge part in it. Putting difficult materials together—like baking something in sunlight, or using one material that fights another material—causes its own organic reaction. Then it's a matter of sitting back and studying it and studying it and studying it; and suddenly, you find you're leaping up out of your chair and going in and doing the next thing. That's action and reaction.

But if you know that you've got to be somewhere in half an hour, there's no way you can achieve that. So the art life means a freedom to have time for the good things to happen. There's not always a lot of time for other things.

I want to close this chapter with a particular perspective on what I've just covered. I provide physical wellness insights in the chapter on Vitality. But I want to share my conviction that structuring your total environ-ment to greatest degree possible, which includes style of dress, décor, music, media, and workshop surround-ings, *keeps you younger.* I do not mean that as a platitude.

In a 2007 study, Harvard psychologist Ellen Langer reported that hotel maids experienced weight loss and reduced blood pressure when taught to understand that their daily work routine had significant aerobic benefits. Once these facts were established, within four weeks subjects lost weight *without changes to their work habits or personal lives,* and compared to no changes in a control group. How they felt about their jobs made a physical dif-ference. In other studies by Langer (these the subject of later controversy but their results never fundamentally refuted) elderly subjects experienced physical and men-tal improvements—including increased muscle mass and flexibility, recovered memory and cognitive func-tion, and improved mood and vitality—when immersed in nostalgic settings filled with stimuli from their youth, including vintage books, music, furnishings, and mov-ies. Settings that evoked feelings of novelty and youth actually seemed to summon the reappearance of youth-ful traits, extending even to improved eyesight.

There are indications that we remain more youthful—not just psychologically but also physically—when possessed of information or surroundings that make us feel so. I have observed this in parents who do not dress and look like parents. I do not mean having a Peter Pan complex, which is embarrassing. I mean retaining a sense of yourself sexually, artistically, stylistically, intellectually, and individually so that you do not slip into a socially conformist mom-and-dad mode. Why is that necessary? In other nations, such as France and Spain, parents do not cease to regard themselves stylistically, artistically, or in matters of personal taste as individuals. They are not consumed by one aspect of their social role.

As I am writing these words in April 2020 I learned of the death of a beloved and groundbreaking clothier on the Lower East Side of Manhattan, Jimmy Webb. Jimmy dressed in a wonderful punk-metal style, wearing all black, leather, boots, chains, studded belts, and other accoutrements. He had the ability to place layer upon layer and make it all seem like part of one canvas. Not crowded, not gaudy, but *e pluribus unum*. He was several years my senior but when people saw him they did not see age. I've similarly noticed that people who are dedicated to the occult or ceremonial magick often seem younger than their years. The same phenomenon is at play: they often dress, stylize, and present themselves in a way that eludes the standard roles and categories we associate with age. This is similar to the marketing executive who I referenced earlier. I believe this effect is palpable.

Look at the photograph on the front of this book. It was taken in New York City around my fifty-fourth birthday in fall 2019. Although the picture was taken by an extraordinary rock photographer, Larry Busacca, it was not touched up or faked in any way. That is me. It is you, too. Claim it.

HABIT 3
RADICAL SELF-RESPONSIBILITY

Look to yourself not exclusively but first.

I f you know my work, you are probably aware that I am a great admirer of the British-Barbadian mystic Neville Goddard (1905–1972), who wrote and spoke on the American metaphysical scene until his death in West Hollywood. Of all the writers to emerge from the alternative spiritual movement of the last century, I consider Neville, who used his first name, as probably the most elegant as a literary figure and communicator. In this regard, he's closely rivaled by Alan Watts.

Neville taught that your imagination is God, and that every reference to God or Christ in Scripture is a symbolic representation of the creative power of thought. In his more than ten books and thousands of lectures, Neville taught that you are a composite of exactly what you believe true of yourself. Your consistent assumptions and mental pictures are your destiny, more than any past or present circumstance. Seen in a certain sense, his message is one of extraordinary self-liberation, and it has been received as such by a vast range of new readers that Neville has attracted in the past fifteen years.

Neville's message is also deeply challenging, especially for those experiencing health difficulties or physical maladies. As I write these words in spring 2020 the world is shaken by coronavirus. Are such things malleable to a change of mentality? And, in the face of chronic pain or other tactilely felt conditions, is a change in psyche even possible? You'll see from my exchange with the reader in the introduction that I not only take these issues with grave seriousness but I believe that we experience many laws and forces, including physical decline and the need for traditional medicine, even if one considers the mind the ultimate arbiter of reality. In my perspective, mental causation is ever-operative. Just like what we call the placebo effect is ever-operative. But intervening factors simultaneously exist. The problem, as I see it, is when we conceive of life as subjected to one mental super law. Because the placebo effect is demonstrably true, for example, I do not expect it to govern all of medicine—although it's a factor.

It is possible that we are unable to experience, from within our present mentality and vantage point, the ultimate role of awareness as the shaper of reality, except in moments of exquisite sensitivity. But this should not serve as a deterrent to personal experiment. Extraordinary events do occur, large and small, and Neville urges you to probe such occurrences for correlation between sustained mental imagery and outer activity.

For the purposes of this volume, I am not going to consider the full metaphysical implications of Neville's thought. Rather, I want to approach his ideas from a different perspective. Every one of us lives by assumptions, whether we acknowledge them. We all harbor untested, psychologically conditioned, and second-hand notions about life, which we seldom scrutinize. Realizing this gives us remarkable freedom to select and road-test different personal and ethical philosophies. That is the spirit in which I hope you will approach this book. You have everything to gain by embracing your freedom to experiment with a new creed. That is what Neville offers.

I invite you to approach Neville's ideas of self-creation, even if for a temporary and fixed period of time, *as though* they are true. This is not because I want you to believe or disbelieve them—that is a matter of your own search. But because they present the seeker with an experiment in radical self-responsibility. How would conduct yourself, how would you measure time, how would you relate to your thoughts, relationships, and circumstances if you were vested with this sense of ultimate creative authority?

Maybe it would make no difference. Maybe we are so imprisoned by the automaticity of emotion, habit, consumption, and conditioning that our behavior wouldn't change at all. The willingness to face that could in itself be revelatory.

One of Neville's qualities that I most love is his challenge to simply *try*. To test his ideas, this very minute, and see if they do not bring results. I believe that electing to follow Neville's way of thought is itself revealing and fortifying. Such a task compels you to look in your own direction in a more steely and ennobling way. I want to share two quotes from Neville's 1941 book *Your Faith is Your Fortune*:

> Change your conception of yourself and you will automatically change the world in which you live. Do not try to change people; they are only messengers telling you who you are. Revalue yourself and they will confirm the change.

> Stop trying to change the world since it is only the mirror. Man's attempt to change the world by force is as fruitless as breaking a mirror in the hope of

changing his face. Leave the mirror and change your face. Leave the world alone and change your conceptions of yourself.

Can't you feel the pulsation of possibility in these ideas? My wish is that *The Miracle Habits* gives you not only the possibility of living from this way of thought but of taking steps that fortify such thoughts. It is unnecessary to accept this on a metaphysical level, unless it helps you in your experiment.

For what I am proposing here, Neville can be seen as a kind of *spiritualized objectivist*. Or perhaps I could say that Ayn Rand, the radical individualist and founder of philosophical objectivism, was a secularized Neville. Neville and Rand each believed, with uncompromising conviction, that the individual creates his own objective reality and circumstances. Rand saw this as a matter of personal will; Neville saw it as a matter of imagination.

I realize that Rand stirs deep feelings in people, often of intense dislike. Please realize that I am not writing about her ideas from political perspective. Rather, I am trying to give a sense of the peak possibility from which you can experiment if you are willing to entertain the thesis of radical self-selectivity. In the final chapter I write about the influence I took from one of Rand's most iconic students, illustrator Steve Ditko.

Try.

*   *   *

At times our minds and emotions are not on the side of our needs, no matter the nature of our mental program or the depth of our efforts. For various reasons, we may experience extended periods of loss and grief, or chronic depression and anxiety. These emotional states can snowball into crises.

Since depression has a complexity of causes—its triggers are often biological and situational—it requires a complexity of treatments: therapeutic, pharmacological, cognitive, meditative, and spiritual. I believe that when contending with depression or other emotional crises no solution should be peremptorily removed from the table. There is no reason why SSRIs or other meds cannot be combined with prayer and spirituality. I take an SSRI myself. It is not something that I want to see stigmatized in the spiritual culture. As I observe later in this chapter, never neglect "established channels," or allow yourself to be made to feel that one approach, such as spirituality, precludes another, such as psycho-pharmacology.

That said, there is no question that American society is facing a current crisis in depression and suicide. "Treatment for chronic depression and anxiety—often the precursors to suicide—has never been more available and more widespread," the *New York Times* noted in June 2018. "Yet the Centers for Disease Control and Prevention this week reported a steady, stubborn rise in the national suicide rate, up 25 percent since 1999."

Since this is a book of motivational philosophy, I will not venture a full analysis of this crisis but I will outline the best that self-development philosophy has to offer, in my estimation, for successfully coping with periods of despair, purposelessness, and grief. To do so, I wish to briefly turn the clock back to when America has been here before. In the mid-1890s, authorities similarly puzzled over a "suicide craze" among young men. The nation was experiencing a period of relative peace and prosperity, and yet states reported a rise in suicides, and newspapers were suffused with daily reports. Then, as today, the suicide index may point to a crisis in social and individual purpose. American philosopher William James (1842–1910) thought so. Indeed, the psychologist had struggled with depression himself—and in response wrote his 1895 lecture and essay, "Is Life Worth Living?"

James argued that we urgently need philosophies of individual purpose and personal intention to counter the impulse that life is not worth living. He was right. Even today we see that social policy and pharmacology—vital as they are—are not sufficient to stem the tide of emotional turmoil. As individuals and as a nation, we must rediscover James's insights. They can save lives. I believe we also need to reduce that stressors people face due to overwork at unsatisfying and low-compensating jobs and an absence of health insurance or the problem of under-insurance. Relieving those burdens can also bolster what James prescribed.

FIGHTING EVIL

"Need and struggle," James wrote, "are what excite and inspire us; our hour of triumph is what brings the void." We are never so strong as when we are actively striving—it is actually the arrival and completion of an aim that seem to deplete our psyche and invite ennui. James's solution? Continual struggle toward worthy ends: "The history of our own race is one long commentary on the cheerfulness that comes with fighting ills." Don't read that in an overly narrow way: Your definition of "fighting ills" may be intimate, such as going through addiction recovery or a personal philosophical experiment. Or it may be public, such as engaging in activism, military or civic service, or starting a constructive business.

The determination is yours, but the message is clear: Fighting evil, however you define it, is vivifying. "Life is worth living," James wrote, "no matter what it brings, if only such combats may be carried to successful terminations and one's heel set on the tyrant's throat."

Working to conquer a problem or ill is the most vital part of living.

REWARD ANTICIPATION

The Victorian age in which James wrote was marked by humanity's newfound understanding of the evolutionary, natural, and biological causes of life. This did not mean abandonment of religion, but it *did* mean that the doctor, minister, or philosopher had to recognize the individual as part of the natural processes of the world. This awareness liberated people to see their lives in their hands. You could, James counseled, take your own life at any time—and that realization itself provides a sense of self-determination: You are not at the mercy of unknowable forces, but you are their final arbiter. Hence, James reasoned, "[W]e can always stand it for twenty-four hours longer, if only to see what tomorrow's newspaper will contain, or what the next postman will bring."

As much as we are victims of repetition and tragedy, we are also, in the course of time, recipients of radically unexpected good news. The miraculous is as much a part of life as the catastrophic. This is lawful. It is not fanciful to wait for welcome and dramatic turns of events; it is practical.

PERSONAL ACHIEVEMENT

James noted that we should never underestimate the need to preserve a sense of personal honor and self-agency. A friend of mine was once depressed when a book he wrote failed to meet sales expectations. Rather than search for some vaguely Eastern form of "nonattachment" or opt for an amorphous search for inner meaning—which can be especially difficult for Westerners—I suggested that he throw himself anew into effort and striving. Does that sound like a corrupted ethic for forever racing on the gerbil wheel of receding achievement? It is not. I specifically question the hallowed expression "no one on his deathbed wishes he had spent more time at the office." Actually, I believe some people find a deep-seated sense of purpose not only at the office, depending on their work, but also the studio, stage, martial arts mat, writer's desk, and so on.

I don't think it helps a disappointed person to discourage his or her return to the workbench; sometimes the workbench is the answer itself. Many people experience a sense of self-realization in entrepreneurship, artistry, and the professions. James grasped this. Too few spiritual thinkers do today.

INDEPENDENT PRAYER

"I confess," James wrote, "that I do not see why the very existence of an invisible world may not in part depend on the personal response which any one of us may make to the religious appeal. God himself, in short, may draw vital strength and increase of very being from our fidelity."

I strongly believe in the power of prayer, devotion, and worship to ease the grip of emotional anguish. When engaging in devotional practices, throw away the rulebook. Pray however you want to whatever greater power you can bring yourself to believe in—even to ethics and rationality. The very act of fealty, James wrote, may serve to increase the presence of productive forces in your life—forces that may direct you to a sought-after answer, insight, sense of personal possibility, and perhaps something more. The book *Alcoholics Anonymous* is especially helpful in this regard.

Childhood conventions or established practices be damned; use James's injunction in the most personal sense. "It is a fact of human nature," he wrote, "that men can live and die by the help of a sort of faith that goes without dogma or definition."

ESCAPING CRUEL PEOPLE

This is one of the centerpieces of this book. In his letters, James noted that "the deepest principle of Human Nature is the craving to be appreciated." The absence of respect and appreciation—and the private toll taken at work and at home by bullies, smart-mouths, gossips, and passive-aggressive creeps—can drive you toward desperation. Indeed, the agonies inflicted by cruel or manipulative people represent an unacknowledged psychosocial crisis; I am convinced this is a factor in despair and suicide.

My heartfelt advice: Cut cruel people out of your life, and burn your bridges behind you. Even if you cannot immediately get away from a destructive personality, begin by doing so as an inner principle. Vow internally to separate as an emotional fact, and then remove yourself from physical proximity at the soonest possible moment. Remember: James called recognition and respect "the deepest principle of Human Nature." Cut ties with those who will not honor it. *This principle is so important that it forms the subject of its own chapter.*

D-DAY APPROACH

James was radically ecumenical in outlook. Take no method, practice, or idea off the table when combatting depression, anxiety, or suicidal thoughts. We are too quick to accept boundaries and limitations in our therapeutic or spiritual search. There exists no reason why you cannot combine spirituality, such as prayer and meditation, with traditional psychopharmacological methods and other forms of talk or cognitive therapy. Take a "Day-D approach": Throw everything you've got at your problem. Listen to no one who insists that one approach precludes another. I know many people who have benefited from a pastiche of drugs, therapy, and the spiritual search, as I have personally.

This is your D-Day—deploy all your resources, and command them like a general. "Be not afraid of life," James concluded in his 1895 essay. "Believe that life is worth living, and your belief will help create the fact."

When facing a predicament, I believe that the individual should, as a first recourse, search within his own person and environment for solutions. Exercise all possibilities. This is not to foster some idealized version of self-reliance or a go-it-alone ethic. Not at all. Rather, locating a lasting personal solution means that you are operating from a sense of abilities, perspective, and agencies that are always within you. A sturdy success will vest you with a validly expanded sense of power. *That does not mean avoiding counsel, therapy, or peer help.* But it raises the bar on your sense of resourcefulness.

In the vein of finding your own solutions, I want to explore a popular exercise I've devised called the 10-Day Miracle Challenge. It is basically an intention experiment in focusing on a single aim. And it has proven powerful. Since I started writing about it, first privately among friends and readers starting in fall of 2018, I have heard from a wide range of people telling me that it worked for them, and often worked on multiple occasions. Here are three representative samples of several dozen:

> Mitch, I met you and heard you speak at the conference at Unity Village in Oct 2019. I participated in your 10-Day Challenge at the beginning of the month. Wow! In those 10 days I brought into being a trip to Amsterdam for an advanced course in my field, a lucrative and rewarding collaboration with a clinic besides my own, and the opportunity to lead some of Florida State University's baseball team in brain balancing work. Once I got focused and consistent, opportunities just snowballed. Thanks for creating the space.
>
> —JERI LaVIGNE, ATLANTA, GA

Dear Mitch, I began my 10-Day Miracle Challenge on January 1st, 2020. My husband and I have been involved in some legal matters I won't go into. My focus for the Miracle Challenge was an end to all of these matters. On the 9th day we received a phone call letting us know everything had been cleared up in a positive way. I'm a believer! I'll be starting another challenge tomorrow. Thank you, Mitch. I'm learning to focus, ask & allow true miracles in my life.

—MELISSA L., NEW ORLEANS, LOUISIANA

Hi Mitch. We've spoken a couple of times and as you know I'm not new to the power of thought in shaping our reality. However, inspired by the immediacy of your 10-Day Miracle Challenge, I turned all my mental resources to settling an outstanding debt. Halfway through the Challenge, I was already halfway to my goal, and by the end of the tenth day I knew for certain that the completion of my goal was within sight. I know mind power is real, but thanks so much for the timely reminder and opening the channels again!

—GREG MOFFITT, YORK, UK,
WWW.LEGALISE-FREEDOM.COM

Before exploring this exercise further—and why it works—let me supply the basics of how to do it:

1. Decide on something that you truly and passion-ately want in your life. Not necessarily your Definite Chief Aim, but something urgently needed, or something that may facilitate your aim.

2. Write it down—your wish should be reducible to one sentence, such as "I have a gainful new job in my field."

3. Set a fixed period of time—in this case 10 days—by which to receive your desire.

4. Draw a grid of 10 boxes and consecutively cross one out each day to mark progress toward your aim.

5. Every day, as often as you can and as much as you can, pray, visualize, affirm, and meditate upon the realization of your wish.

6. Finally—and here is the most important part—watch very carefully for the arrival of your aim; *take care not to overlook or discount the means by which it arrives.*

*   *   *

Why should any of this work? For me, the 10-Day Miracle Challenge is something of an adjunct to sigil magick. I wasn't thinking of sigil magick when I created it, but later it struck me that the challenge resolves some of my personal difficulties in working with sigil magick.

For those of you haven't heard of it, or who have heard the term but don't know much about what it means, sigil magick is the central practice of what is called chaos magick. English artist, occultist, and visionary Austin Osman Spare (1886–1956) pioneered the method. Sigil magick involves reworking a written sentence of your desire into an abstract symbol, focusing on the symbol while in an ecstatic state, and then letting it all go. That process unleashes the creative energies of your wish.

In its most popular form (and there are limitless variations), the operation goes like this: You write a plain sentence of your desire, such as: "I have a beautiful new home nearby my work." You then use a process of letter elimination to reduce your sentence to a non-intelligible series of letters. A common practice is to eliminate all repeating letters. Your statement would then appear this way: "Ihavebutflhomnrywk."

You then arrange each remaining letter, one by one, into an abstract sigil with no expository meaning. If I assemble the letters above into a sigil it might look like this:

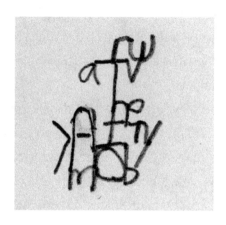

The final part of the procedure is to "charge" your sigil. To do this, you effectively stop thinking of your desire, accepting that your desire is now represented entirely by the sigil you have created. You bring yourself into a state of ecstasy or non-ordinary consciousness— usually through self-pleasured orgasm (or sometimes dancing, meditating, taking drugs or any other activity that works for you)—while focusing on your sigil. You concentrate on your sigil at the moment of climax, and then forget all about it. You are done.

The principle is that by transferring your wish onto the sigil and thus charging it, you have eluded the rational apparatus of the mind. You are no longer "in desire," which is a feeling of want but not fulfillment, and you have allowed the sigil itself, through climax, to enter into the subconscious reaches of your mind, and thus be joined to the transcendent channels of causative intelligence. Some people offer different explanations, but I think this is a fair representation of what "happens" in sigil magick.

I know many capable and gifted people who report extraordinary results with this method. But, as much as I respect and admire this practice (I even have a sigil tattooed on the back of my neck), I have not, as of this writing, personally experienced success with it.* I have wondered why this is so. It may be because I experience difficulty with one of the key facets of sigil magick, which is *purposeful forgetting.* You are not to dwell on your desire. You are not to remain in a state of hope or wanting. Rather, you are to transfer your desire onto your sigil, and through the process of concentrated climax you effectively satisfy your desire. Or so the method goes. At this point you are done. The work is finished. The desire is realized.

This approach has psychological similarities with aspects of New Thought and specifically with the sys-

---

* Although I must add this addendum: soon after "charging" the sigil in this book, I contracted a mild case of coronavirus which kept me homebound for several weeks, during which time I worked prodigiously and also tidied and arranged my apartment. You could say I had gotten the beautiful home—very near to my work!

tem of mystic Neville Goddard. Neville told students to "live from the end" of the desire fulfilled. Imagine how you would feel, he said, if what you want has already come to pass. Both systems, Neville's and sigil magick, require an assumption of the wish fulfilled. Neville allows for somewhat greater flexibility insofar as he acknowledged that this may be a repeat process. You will inevitably snap to awareness that your desire has *not* arrived. Hence, Neville taught that you might have to repeat a visualizing procedure night after night. Persistence and gestation are part of his system.

As noted, I think this process of transfer and forgetting has been a personal barrier to me. It is not in my rational (and over-eager) nature to simply "forget about it." This has proven a blockage in ritual of any kind that is designed to unburden me of desire.

Magician, artist, and Church of Satan founder Anton LaVey has written perceptively about this problem. In his essay "Ravings from Tartarus" from his collection, *The Devil's Notebook*, Anton explored the question of why a ritual doesn't seem to work. "Because it matters so much to you," he replied.

Anton believed that a ritual or ceremony should immerse you in feeling *satisfied* that you have gained the thing wished for. In this regard, sexuality and self-sexuality were core tools in his ritualistic system. Once you experience the longed-for sense of satedness, you drop the matter. "Burn every bit of desire out of your system," Anton wrote, "and then, when you no longer care, it will come to you."

If you don't experience satisfaction, your fantasy or ritual must be performed again. Or, you must find another way of diverting yourself from futile distraction with your aim. Again, Anton:

How can one avoid caring? There are many tricks which can be employed. Creativity is one. When you are in the process of creating something your brain must function on a creative level, not on a rote or repetitive one. Your mind cannot be possessed by one thing and yet entertain new thoughts—unless the object of your creation happens to be in the likeness of your obsession. Here we find an ideal combination, for if the hands can create a facsimile of the desired objective with such dexterity as to be convincing then it is as good as done.

Anton supplied a good method for diversion. Again, the point of chaos magick, sigil work, and related techniques is to bypass the rational apparatus of the mind and allow the depths of the subconscious—which is, I believe, the medium that allows us to select among different realities—to do its work.

If you're like me, however, this bypassing may prove a barrier. I think eagerly and continually about my wishes. I cannot "forget" or transfer them. At least not so far in my search. Magickal partners have chided me about this quality—but it persists. And this is where the 10-Day Miracle Challenge enters.

I do not believe there is any sole way to approach New Thought, magick, ritual, affirmation, prayer, or spell work. Call it whatever you will, all of these methods involve externalizing and concretizing your wishes, stirring up and employing the causative or selective agencies of the mind.* Some writers and practitioners insist that the royal road to mental or psychical causation necessarily involves working around, not through, the rational mind. But I am not sure that is correct. Based on personal results and observations, I believe that we can also employ these psychical energies through consciously aware means. Our lives are, I believe, physical and extra-physical; five-sensory and extra-sensory; linear and infinite; material and transcendent. You are not bound by any one approach in exploring and exercising the fullness of your nature.

Hence, the 10-Day Miracle Challenge offers a way of identifying and actualizing your desires that does

---

* I theorize the mechanics behind this process in *The Miracle Club, One Simple Idea,* and *Magician of the Beautiful.*

not require forgetting, displacing, or rearranging them. Rather, you concentrate upon your desires fully—but with a special kind of vigilance.

Here is part of the mysterious but pivotal nature of this exercise. When the things you wish for arrive, it is often *in a form that you do not expect*, do not necessarily recognize, and that you might discount either because the arrival seems too mundane or too different from the expected outcome.

The likelihood is that whatever reaches you will arrive through some kind of *established channel*. Working with established lines is one of the subtlest and most important points in magick. It means that you must pay attention to practical, even if unexpected, avenues of fulfillment. Wallace D. Wattles makes this point his 1910 classic *The Science of Getting Rich*:

In creating, the Formless seems to move according to the lines of motion it has established; the thought of an oak tree does not cause the instant formation of a full-grown tree, but does start in motion the forces which will produce the tree, along established lines of growth. Every thought of form, held in thinking Substance, causes the creation of the form, but always, or at least generally, along lines of growth and action already established. The thought of a house of a certain construction, if it were impressed upon Formless

92

Substance, might not cause the instant formation of the house; but it would cause the turning of creative energies already working in trade and commerce into such channels as to result in the speedy building of the house. And if there were no existing channels through which the creative energy could work, then the house would be formed directly from primal substance without waiting for the slow processes of the organic and inorganic world.

In practical terms, this means that your goal is likely to arrive through preexisting paths. For example, if you seek the cure of an illness, the likelihood is not that your illness will spontaneously lift, but rather that you will discover a network of treatments that produce recovery. If you are looking for work, the overwhelming odds are that you will make connections and find ideas and leads that will deliver you to what you need—less likely is that someone will walk up and hand you, signed and sealed, the desired offer.

Some practitioners of chaos or sigil magick take this principle a step further. When prescribing a spell or ceremony—which is really a ritualized intention, no different from positive-mind or New Thought methods— they insist that, in order for such operations to work, there must be a clear means of arrival. For example, if you wish for love but dwell as a shut-in there is no obvious channel of delivery. But if you wish for love and actively circulate among people, you are providing an established channel for fulfillment. (This is also a key principle for cultivating good luck—a topic for another day.)

Each individual must study and consider this step for him or herself. Are you asking for something that fits the context of your life, practices, and habits? Is there a foreseeable means of delivery? Or, put from a different perspective, are you neglecting or overlooking patterns of delivery—or perhaps the very arrival of what you want simply because it reaches you in unfamiliar ways?

Beware the familiar. Earlier I quoted the spiritual thinker David Spangler, who honed some of his insights while working at the innovative mystical community Findhorn in Northern Scotland in the early 1970s. The Findhorn community used New Thought methods to fuel its remarkable growth and self-sustainability. Referring to the community's cofounder Peter Caddy, Spangler wrote in *The Laws of Manifestation*:

> Peter would say that the good was the enemy of the best and that we should not settle for less than what will do the job perfectly. But sometimes the familiar is the enemy of the possible. We may form images on the basis of what we already know or what we think is possible, neither of which may be the best solution to the need we want to fulfill through manifestation.

What we expect can easily blind us to what can actually drive us toward success; the arrival may come not as the *thing* that what we want but the *condition* that we need. Here is an old joke that drives home this point. During a massive flood a clergyman fled to the roof of his church to avoid being swept away in the waters. A man in a raft came by and told him to come aboard. The clergyman refused. "God will save me," he said. Someone rowed by in a boat and urged him to come on it. But again the clergyman refused. "God will save me," he said. Finally, a helicopter appeared overhead and dropped a ladder. But the man waved it away. "God will save me!" he yelled. The floodwaters eventually overtook the clergyman and he drowned. Upon reaching heaven he protested to God, "I've served you all my life! Why didn't you save me?" To which God replied: "I didn't save you? I sent the raft, I sent the boat, I sent the helicopter . . ."

The lesson is: Remain open. Take the road when it appears. Reject nothing out of hand. And *never* neglect established means. What you need, whether a condition or a thing, may arrive in ways that you've dismissed, sworn off, or overlooked. I believe this is one of the many meanings found in ancient parables of travelling strangers who turn out to be deities, kings, or supernatural messengers in disguise. They shower gifts upon those who invite them in.

HABIT 4

SOLIDARITY

Deeds not words.

---

wrote earlier about freeing yourself from the need to couch your Definite Chief Aim in terms of service. In 2020 I heard from a friendly critic who believed that I paid too little attention to the need for service. He wrote:

It seems the drive toward power is indeed in us all. Further growth of and exercise of one's abilities also seems to have some kind of intrinsic benefit. But it also seems striving in the absence of some externally provided goals ends up vacuous and unsatisfying. We were built to work in service of something larger than ourselves, in which we believe.

It seems you are trying to deny this second impulse. It seems there are many broken people down that path.

I responded:

After many years on the spiritual path I've grown suspicious of terms like "service," which accrue virtue to the user but are often wielded with subtle judgment, as you do here. If a person behaves in a generative and productive way, acting with reciprocity and transparency, that seems to me "service" enough, and a measurable benefit to others. Conversely, many self-proclaimed spiritual people, who provide few such benefits, conceal selfishness or fecklessness behind tributes to service.

I have witnessed numerous episodes where New Age and spiritual organizations whose marketing materials, websites, and internal culture make paeans to service, social responsibility, and conscious business do everything possible to avoid or delay paying artists, presenters, and vendors, and who have even lost discrimination suits (in one case, shockingly, firing two employees recovering from the same illness several years apart). These anecdotal experiences are, of course, no argument against a seemingly age-old ethic like service. But what *is* service? Is it necessary to a well-lived and powerful life? I pose that question not to sound heterodox but only because I believe we must explore these concepts freshly rather than accept handed-down definitions.

If your concept of service means aiding others, under what circumstances and how? A wise person once said, "The only things you can really give another person are time or money." It's one of those statements that immediately begs argument. This is because it is shockingly true and cuts away fantasy. I used to witness someone who wore a mink coat to a New Thought church and when the collection basket came around instead of dropping in bills or a check she waved her hand over it and uttered an incantation. You do not have to give. The yoga of money can mean giving or not giving. But be clear about it.

The publisher of this book, a man of genuine philanthropic bent, told me that an early draft neglected mention of giving back. Hence, I endeavored to ask myself what that concept means. We're all bound up in complex motives—often denying the wish for self-gain but nonetheless harboring it. More important than the motivation is concreteness of benefit. Years ago I was in a copy shop and the owner was telling me that his mother was a psychic. He was obviously proud of her and repeated for me some of her principles. One of them was that even if you're doing something generous in order to look good or curry favor, if the end result still benefits another person then your act is a net positive.

A related but somewhat different teaching appears in traditional Judaism. The twentieth-century theologian Rabbi Abraham Joshua Heschel (1911–1972) once took up the question of sincerity in charitable acts. Heschel was asked whether a person must have the right motive when giving. The rabbi taught that the act is more important than the motive. He said that if you perform an ethically powerful act, even without a sincere motive or with a mixed motive, your feeling state will eventually come into alignment with the nature of the act. Heschel's point was that actions are paramount. It is not always possible to understand a motive, even your own. Let the act take precedence.

Within the New Thought culture there exist many teachings about tithing, an ancient religious practice once designed to support temple orders and religious communities through the giving of ten-percent of one's earnings or goods. The Old Testament teaches that the tithe-giver receives multiple rewards in exchange. "Honor the Lord with your wealth, with the first fruits of all your crops; then your barns will be filled to over-

flowing, and your vats will brim over with new wine."
(Proverbs 3:9–10) This outlook is echoed in some Christian denominations today, and especially in certain reaches of the Prosperity Gospel and New Thought.

I have personally experimented with tithing. If it is meaningful in the life of an individual then I have no argument with it. For me, it was not. The problem with modern tithing is that, like the sometimes-deflective use of the term service, I believe it encourages concealed self-gain. Concealment is not a means to growth. Nearly every New Thought minister or writer who encourages tithing, from Edwene Gaines to Catherine Ponder, insists that it must be done with no strings attached, with love, without selfishness. But the practice is nonetheless a quid pro quo. This is the kind of act—thinking one way ("I'm doing this with love") and feeling another, however covertly ("I hope this pays off")—is the kind of attitude that can tear the seeker in two, similar to the discord around nonattachment versus attainment.

Like many who speak openly of their virtues, those who talk publicly about tithing in reality often have a fitful relationship to it, like buying a piece of home exercise equipment that becomes a towel rack. I've never solicited a tithe (which would be gross), but I've had the experience of people volunteering to me that they are sending me a tithe and do not. I've witnessed ministers and churches send tithes to widely known figures and then get angry when those figures don't agree to speak at their church. Again, the strings of expectation are felt but unspoken. I write this sympathetically: I have tithed and found that it was nearly impossible to separate myself from expectation of a payback, which is the chief reason why tithing is popular within prosperity circles. And why shouldn't you expect a payback? It's human nature.

I hope this segment doesn't insult those who tithe in good faith. They certainly exist. I'm only sharing my observations and not attempting a blanket judgment. (In fact, I'm happy to hear from readers who have had positive experiences with tithing) The point is: I want concepts of giving and service done with transparency, self-honesty, and realness—not as a concealed piece of self-seeking. Self-seeking is not the problem. The problem is obfuscation.

I believe that one of the ways in which we can pursue genuine solidarity is through loyalty to friends, collaborators, and workmates, especially when they are in duress. I find it odd how little we hear today about loyalty as a virtue. In the primeval world, loyalty stood as one of the defining traits of life—loyalty to tribe, pack, family, friend, and community. Today the ideal is seen

as quaint if not backwards. Many people on hearing the
term *loyalty* sniff something unhealthy in it and are apt
to ask rhetorically, "Should I be loyal to a bad boss? A
crook? A lousy friend?" No, you shouldn't. That would
be an act of corruption. Loyalty is not groupthink or
servility. Rather, it is reciprocity, reliability, and cama-
raderie. You do not avert your eyes from a colleague in
trouble. You do not gloat, however insidiously or internally, over someone's suffering. You do not immediately
accept summary or group judgments. If a person dwells
within your circle of friends, workmates, and community (however broadly defined), you start from a place
of solidarity and protectiveness. You give succor so that
person knows he or she is not abandoned when injured.
You join someone's side. You'll need the same sooner
than you think.

Displaying solidary forms around you a community of nobility and reciprocity. If you have the back
of a sound and mature person, there is a reasonable
likelihood that your display will come back to you and
put you in the debt of a circle of capable people. This
is not a cynical ploy, though it is self-interested; it is
also group-interested. It requires identifying who you
view as a true friend and colleague. Solidary and loyalty lift burdens from others; make them feel seen and
protected; and, as noted earlier, your motives may be
mixed (as most motives are) but you are signaling a

union of support to people you view as comrades. Never neglect how important that can be, or how much safety it can give you.

For all the talk of money and time, I am not blind to people's emotional needs. I believe that one of the most important acts of reciprocity you can make is to attempt to genuinely see others.

Few things in life are more painful than not being seen. Recognizing someone in both achievement and in suffering provides that person with an enormously powerful release from emotional loneliness. Conversely, denying another's pain or, even worse, gaslighting that person and masking your role in it, is among the lowest and most dishonorable forms of the behavior. No amount of hours "saving the world" or tweeting about it erases the emotional violence that type of behavior does.

I believe that many people suffer lingering anguish and trauma from emotional, sexual, or physical abuse not solely because of the events themselves but because those close to them, especially parents and caregivers, never acknowledge what occurred. Even if a given parent or guardian wasn't the offending party, they still owe it to kids, including grown kids, to recognize what transpired, and, if the situation calls for it, to own up to whether they did all they could to have protected the child or prevented the situation. Feeling seen and acknowledged, at any age, is the most powerful salve for trauma. But withholding a sincere apology or recognition, or worse still denying another's suffering, turns trauma into a chronically unhealed injury.

A magnificent screen example of the power of recognition and acknowledgement of trauma appears in the 2001 Bollywood romantic comedy *Monsoon Wedding*. Although I call the film a comedy it is much more than that. (Spoiler: I reveal the ending in this description.) The events unfold around a lavish wedding in Delhi, in which a modern Indian family is struggling with the expenses of marrying their daughter. The householder Lalit is well off but nonetheless under financial strain as family from all over the world descend on his home and last-minute expenses pile up. Lalit and others glow with respect at the arrival of his wealthy, American-dwelling brother-in-law Tej, who has been a financial support to the family. One person, however, shrinks from Tej, Lalit's adult niece, Ria, who has lived with the family since the death of her father.

Ria soon notices Tej taking a flirtatious interest in a 10-year-old relative, Aliya. During an evening of pre-wedding festivities Ria spies Tej attempting to drive away with Aliya. She throws herself in front of the car to stop him and reveals the truth: Tej sexually abused Ria as a girl. Ria puts herself on the line to prevent this pattern from repeating. Some family members accuse Ria of lying, and say that as an unmarried woman she's just vindictive and bitter on the wedding eve. Lalit and his wife trust Ria, but their defense of her is muted and they are eager to avoid insulting the wealthy Tej. Ria flees the home. The following day, Lalit, still divided, pleads with Ria to return, which she does. Shortly before the wedding ceremony, the family is gathered before a small shrine to honor Ria's father. Lalit, in a moment of quiet but profound bravery, tells his benefactor Tej that he must leave their home. He stands up for Ria. As Tej departs, a tremendous burden is lifted from Ria—and 10-year-old Aliya is protected. The cycle has been broken. Ria is free. For me, it is one of the most subtly powerful and revealing moments in cinema.

If you want bravery, if you want to know what solidarity means, look at the characters of Lalit and Ria. They don't carry guns, wear costumes, or fly into battle—and they are some of the finest heroes that recent cinema has produced. Lalit cannot undo the past—or can he? The spiritual teacher G.I. Gurdjieff observed that the past controls the future, but the present controls the past. This can be understood on several levels. Here is one: the meaning ascribed to the past, and our response to it in the present, shapes the nature of the past. In *The Miracle Club*, I raise the question of whether our limited understanding of the nature of time might conceal that through our perspective we are constantly changing, or selecting, the past.

Few things in life are more painful than not being seen. Victims of physical, verbal, or emotional abuse often dwell less on the events themselves than on the lack of understanding, or the willful denial, demonstrated by others. As I explore in the chapter on Cruel People, tormenters often possess plausible denial—they cultivate it. This allows them to maintain a curtain of concealment around their actions. Plausible denial is a bastard cousin to gaslighting. If a victim cannot be seen, his or her suffering chronically festers. For this reason I believe the nation of South Africa performed a profoundly important service following apartheid when it conducted Truth and Reconciliation Commission hearings throughout the country from 1995 to 2002. These hearings allowed witnesses and victims the opportunity to describe and document human-rights violations.

When people's need to be seen is denied, their pain gets perpetuated in sometimes unexpected and schismatic ways. For example, a wave of fictitious "Satanic abuse" scandals spread across the U.S. in the 1980s and 90s, engulfing and destroying the lives of many innocent people who were falsely accused of salacious and absurd acts of ritual abuse. Some media, courts, police, and not-very-discriminating therapists and self-anointed specialists fanned the flames of sensationalism and calumny. Some of the abuse claimants, who were manipulated or egged on by gung-ho "advocates," probably were victims of actual abuse at the hands of family members, caregivers, or ministers. Yet they were so often ignored, unprotected, and desperate to be heard that they got roped into a false storyline. In that sense, some were made victims twice; and they, in turn, made victims of the wrongly accused. This is the vicious cycle that can occur when people are unseen.

Survivors of childhood abuse often recall the manner in which their claims were initially dismissed, especially within institutions charged to protect them. During the years that the Satanic abuse narrative played out in the media, look at what was actually occurring: chronic and systematically concealed or under-reported cases of sexual abuse in the Catholic Church and the Boy Scouts of America, groups seen as the polar opposite of robe-wearing Satanists. As of this writing the Boy Scouts of America has declared bankruptcy to shield itself from survivor lawsuits. More than twenty Catholic dioceses or religious orders have filed for bankruptcy amid abuse claims. As often occurs in history, we displace stories of abuse from one source to a polar opposite, and in the process create scapegoats, such as the witch in the middle ages or the ritual Satanist in the 1980s and 90s.

You interrupt such cycles and practice reciprocity by performing the solidaristic act of simply *listening to people,* with maturity, realness, and compassion. And when rightly called upon *to act*—to place a sense of responsibility above convenience, self-gain, or a guild mentality.

HABIT 5

HONORABLE SPEECH

---

*Disrespect and blather
have no place in your life.*

One of the comments that has meant the most to me in my career came after the paperback publication of my book on the history of positive thinking, *One Simple Idea*. I was delivering a talk at a sports memorabilia firm in Westchester County, New York. Every employee was in attendance from warehouse workers to salespeople. After the presentation a salesman approached me and said, "I really want to thank you for being here. Most of the speakers who come here tell us how to get people to like us so we can sell them more stuff. You gave us a sense of what we owe to ourselves."

I was moved by what he said because I believe that positive-mind philosophy is about more than just being a better account executive or salesperson, although those things are very important. But what matters most is personal honor. The path to honor and nobility is often as simple as what you say and do not say, whether in person, in writing, or on social media.

I often inveigh against gossip. This does not mean remaining silent in the face of injustice. It means disengaging from spreading idle rumors and speculative ugliness for reasons of titillation, hostility, or entertainment (the three are often bound up), whether in conversation or media. I vow to you that nothing will make you stand taller, and do so more quickly, than desisting from this kind of activity. Engaging in gossip and rumor degrade you as much as consuming something mildly poisonous. And the effects are cumulative.

This is because of how gossip conditions us. You can only see those traits in others that you harbor in yourself. Hence a dishonest person does not recognize honesty in another; he sees it as weakness. Since gossip is almost always in the negative we are, in effect, talking about traits that we harbor and engaging in subtle but definite degradation of self. This is why you probably feel physically exhausted and anxious after an hour spent gossiping. If there exists a human polity or wholeness then it stands to reason that all of our remarks are ultimately self-directed. I believe there is a metaphysical dimension to reciprocity, which provides an esoteric dimension to the Golden Rule, so named in late seventeenth-century England.

I advise you to read Napoleon Hill's chapter on the Golden Rule from his 1928 book *The Law of Success*. Hill's insight on the Golden Rule deserves emphasis and renewed attention. When Hill adapted his first round of teachings from *The Law of Success* into the more compact *Think and Grow Rich* almost ten years later he omitted his chapter on the Golden Rule. I regret his choice. His 1928 chapter opened a window on this familiar but underestimated principle.

Hill argued that the Golden Rule applies not only to what you do to others but also to what you think about them. He wrote that the process of auto-suggestion—which means the suggestions we make to ourselves—gets set in motion by every thought that you accept about self or another, which forms a part of your essential character. That makes the Golden Rule a more urgent principle than we realize.

"We have always been inescapably involved in common destiny," Hill wrote. I believe in that statement. Life is reciprocal. I have never personally witnessed happy endings in the lives of people whose successes or victories were attained by stepping on the skulls of others. I've known people who attained wealth or comfort unscrupulously, without attention to ethics or transparency; I have known people who won temporary victories by smearing the reputations of others; I have known people who made formidable Monday-morning warriors but who lacked dignity and nobility. In my observation, as the years pass, such people are almost always skittish, angry, uneasy, suspicious, and, ultimately, alone.

There exists a ledger of payback for one's behavior because, as Hill observed, we enact in ourselves the circumstances that we perceive in the world. Perception is largely a matter of choice. As alluded, we're incapable of recognizing a virtue in another that we do not possess ourselves. Hence, perspective and character are one whole. You are what you see and see what you are. Observe life carefully and purposefully. Do not submit to prejudice or rote thinking.

The next time you are tempted to repeat a smear about a workmate, acquaintance, neighbor, or family member, ask yourself: Do I know this is true? Have I witnessed any of this firsthand? Moreover, ask: Have I read the book of this person's life? Do I know whether there may exist a network of mitigating circumstances of which I am unaware? Determine whether to repeat something only after asking these questions.

Next to abstaining from gossip, the simplest and most immediate step you can take to uplift your sense of self-respect and how others see you is to stop complaining. Complaining consumes an enormous amount of our everyday speech and conversation. So much so that we do not even notice it—until we attempt to stop.

Most us harbor the illusion that we can reduce our discomforts, petty and otherwise, by talking about them. This may provide temporary relief, especially when friends rush to agree with us. And sometimes this kind of venting is necessary, especially when solving a problem or trying to sort out a conflict. But often such talk creates a spiral of repetition that engulfs our lives.

I know people whose every utterance is some variation of a complaint: about poor service in a restaurant, about the weather, about their neighbors, about the slowness of a train or elevator, about traffic, about the argument they just had, about being misunderstood, about every offense or inconvenience, large or small, real or imagined. I have relatives for whom life consists of a total of about twenty complaints repeated over and over with slight variation. Literally. Living in one of the wealthiest societies in the world, this is not only self-pitying but also corrupt.

Many of us get conditioned into this kind of talking from a young age. It is only when you make an effort to control these statements that you discover how common they are. You may find that you cannot control them. Or that you do not want to control them. There is a certain thrill in anger and complaining. But if you slowly excise the pettiest complaints you will discover that a subtle but unmistakable strength accrues to you when you do not complain, or do so infrequently. You will also find that others are more apt to solicit your point of view, and to listen more carefully or immediately when you talk.

People have long criticized Victorian culture for its repressiveness, discouragement of honest dialogue, and prejudice. All those things are true, to greater or lesser degrees. But in our contemporary world I believe we would benefit from regaining a sliver of the stoic solemnity idealized, if not always practiced, in Victorian culture.

A good example—one that is not maudlin or stereotypical—is Ford Maddox Ford's character Christopher Tietjens, a misunderstood, principled statistician and British officer surrounded by an insincere and crumbling World War I social order in Ford's series of experimental novels *Parade's End* (1924–1928). If your reading taste in modernist experimentalism has its limits, playwright Tom Stoppard adapted Ford's tetralogy into a chronologically linear and compelling miniseries of the same name.

All of the performances evince subtle brilliance, but Benedict Cumberbatch's depiction of the tormented hero Tietjens is among the most memorable screen portrayals I've seen. Tietjens withstands being misunderstood without repeating himself or justifying himself. Cumberbatch's performance may give you a morale boost for the effort I am describing. His character exemplifies a sense of constructive manhood and of desisting from complaint in favor of action, even at the risk of being misunderstood. Tietjens suffers in reputation—but is ultimately understood among people who truly matter to him.

A lot of what I am writing here is about the destructive nature of misdirected anger and powerlessness. It took me too long in life to learn how damaging it is to take an angry tone with people. I grew up thinking that was how men talk. Archie Bunker (who seems perfectly fuzzy and lovable compared to today's politics) seemed entirely normal to me. I heard such tones from my father, and I'm sure he heard it from his. But I did not hear how I sounded to others. I did not hear myself. When you speak angrily to people they are frightened and humiliated. They never forget it. I often say that when you insult or humiliate someone, even indirectly, you will forget about it a lot sooner than they will. You have not only hurt someone but made a lifelong enemy.

To the aggressor, anger is intoxicating. You may have noticed, as I did as an adolescent, that when you vent anger at someone they are sometimes shocked, and they back down from whatever (usually minor) dispute is occurring. It is the worst possible kind of reinforcement because it persuades the aggressor of his or her success.

One of the greatest regrets of my life is the tone of anger that I not infrequently brought into my household. As is universally the case, my children, to a greater or lesser degree, learned from it and I have spent the better part of their adolescence attempting to model a different kind of behavior. Nothing is more corrosive of the human situation—socially, politically, commercially, and intimately—than purposeless anger.

It is often said that anger is fear. That is probably true. But anger's effects are more of what concerns me. In that vein, anger or hostility can take many different forms. Among the worst, as noted in the segment on Solidarity, are acts of gaslighting, undermining cracks, backhanded compliments, and unwillingness to recognize other people's needs or their trauma.

I greatly admire a spiritual teacher named Vernon Howard (1918–1992), who began writing more or less in the New Thought vein and later evolved into a remark-able and unclassifiable metaphysical thinker. Vernon was known for his very direct and sometimes pugna-cious style. But he always had a purpose. One night he erupted at a roomful of students: "What I'm really trying to say is, why don't you just *leave people alone*? They've got problems of their own. They don't need your jokes or your smart remarks."

As was often the case with Vernon, he would say seemingly simple things that concealed great dimen-sions of truth. Imagine how transformative it would be if we really understood what it meant to "leave people alone"—not to bother, harass, impinge on, or burden other people with superfluous comments, wisecracks, unnecessary requests, or angry demands. Vernon said that you can begin to learn the meaning of self-sufficiency and nonviolence (emotional or physical) by taking responsibility for yourself in very simple tasks, including around the household. For example, before asking someone where the scissors are, where the tape is, look for these things yourself. Before asking some-one to fetch something for you, get it yourself. Nine out of ten times you don't need to distract another person. Small steps are revealing.

Vernon used to teach that we mask our hostility in myriad ways. Including what is sometimes called incompetence. In a contentious but, I think, brilliant insight, Vernon taught that we should understand incompetence as hostility because *it has the same effects as hostility.* The incompetent person makes others nervous and agitated; makes them work harder; withholds legitimate goods or cooperation; and demands undeserved rewards. Vernon would always teach that you should watch for the effects—and within them you will detect the motives. In that sense, he viewed hostility as the central malady of the human condition.

In another controversial teaching, Vernon would say, "Show me the victim and I'll show you the bully." He insisted that most of our personal predicaments are self-selected, however subtly we conceal this (including from ourselves), and that people often cry victimhood as an excuse to assail others. It is difficult to swallow such a teaching and easy to name exceptions. There *are* people who have veritably suffered. At the same time, it is a powerful teaching to experiment with. I've known individuals who moan about all that's being done to them, who seem perpetually afraid, anxious, and under threat—yet these same people are some of the worst gossips I've ever encountered. They experience the world as threatening (as gossipers often do), but they use that fear as a platform to debase others. Whatever the root cause, the effect is one of harm.

I realize that some of this sounds harsh. When one of my kids was very young he took one of my notebooks and surreptitiously wrote in it, "Vernon Howard is mean!" (He had overhead recordings of some of Vernon's lectures.) But I explained that Vernon meant these provocations as a way to think freshly about the problems of human nature. We are not always who we say we are, including to ourselves. And we can begin to see this by noting the effects that we have on others. Often in our anger, fear, and hostility—and very often through verbiage—we act out the kinds of emotional violence toward others that we believe we oppose.

Random opinions are a form of hostility if expressed with pushiness. Most people know very little about anything outside of their immediate experience. But something in our conditioning encourages us to hold forth about all kinds of things that we know little or nothing about in matters of money, politics, health, child-raising, education, and you name it.

Napoleon Hill cautioned to protect yourself from the random opinions of others. He taught that your aim and your most valued projects should be shared only with trusted partners and collaborators, and with people who demonstrably know what they are talking about. If you offer up your plans to just anyone—including friends, workmates, and dinner-party guests—you will almost always get an earful of unsolicited advice or judgments from people who have little or no experience with what you're working on. If you idly share your cherished plans or projects, maybe seeking approval from others, you will get thrown off your game by hearing from people who have zero expertise in your field and who plant unwarranted seeds of doubt. Even experts get things wrong. Brilliant people are wrong all the time. Probably four out of five times. Product research gets things wrong. Remember New Coke, Web TV, Google Glass, and Zima? If product researchers are wrong and if brilliant people are wrong then why should you trust someone's random point of view?

Moreover, why even offer a random point of view? I once listened in inebriated boredom while a real-estate attorney explained to me everything that was wrong with the layout of a brilliantly produced and innovative magazine. When you show a new project or a work-in-progress—including a poster, book cover, website, or publication—to a random person they will almost always supply a random point of view. Only true artists and creatives know how to either evaluate something as good or offer a means of improvement, and leave it at that. Most people feel impelled to make comments that show how "creative" they are. If you wouldn't trust a stranger to fix your car, diagnose your symptoms, or upholster your sofa why would you trust your writing, clothing, career dream, or anything of value to whomever happens to be seated next to you? Praise is a mark of intelligence; do not withhold it. It shows the ability to value effort. Criticism should be offered only when specific, practical, based on experience—and requested.

Never undermine your sense of truth, your ideas, or your language in pleas for popularity or acceptance. In a world of instant posting, addictive "likes," and tabulated followings it is easy to succumb to generating click-bait articles or posts, using snarky-funny language, or racing to the common low point for audience share. There are financial rewards to this, too. I find them tempting myself. But I must advise: always place posterity before popularity.

First off, popularity is fleeting. Anyone who has mastered whatever the current vernacular is will soon be yesterday's news, literally and figuratively. Every living writer who has inspired me has written things that I believe will stay around long after his or her demise. In the medium run, cultivation of quality will also pay you more.

More importantly, there is a vital and unseen connection between quality of language and quality of thought. When you stoop to perpetual sarcasm, in-the-know language, or political talking points you ensure conformity. Originality resists rote language. There exists a degenerative symbiosis between groupspeak and groupthink. If you want to glow as a writer, thinker, or communicator, write like *you* talk—not like *they* talk.

One night at a party I was listening to hip-hop artist contrast the art scene in Baltimore, where he lived, with the art scene in Los Angeles. I listened with rapt attention—everything he said was totally original. It was based on personal experience, up-close observation, and couched in a distinct style of putting things. It was one of the most nonconformist descriptions I had ever heard. I wish I had gotten his name. It came out of direct contact with the worlds he was observing. Again, Emerson: "imitation is suicide."

This raises an adjunct point. Never hide being educated or intellectually accomplished, in whatever form that takes, including street cred. Never alter or dumbdown your manner, either because you're afraid of seeming *bourg* (what could be more *bourg* than that?), or because you want to be more appealing. I hate it whenever a producer or editor cautions me not to be "too intellectual." That is pure bullshit. I won't work with such people. Intellectual doesn't mean ineffectual. Or unpopular. Anyone who thinks so has nothing to offer.

I once wrote a television treatment for a docu-series about one of my true heroes, ESP researcher J.B. Rhine (1895–1980). Rhine and his wife and intellectual partner Louisa labored for decades at Duke University to raise the standard on study of the paranormal. My writing partner kept warning me not to be too intellectual; instead, go for the boldface names, be more sensational. I complied. After we handed over the treatment to a production company we got a rejection from a network and the production company basically dropped us.

Weeks later when I revisited the treatment I felt almost physically ill. There was nothing strictly untrue in it. I didn't fudge any facts. But I saw that in my zeal to please others I had raced to the bottom: I told the story as gaudily as possible. In so doing, I disregarded the very thing that made J.B. Rhine a hero to me: his conservative realism, intellectual solidity, and rejection of unprincipled compromise. That's what inspired me to become a historian of alternative spirituality, and to write in the field of the occult and metaphysical. Like J.B., I wanted to bring intellectual excellence to an area where it was in need. I let slide those principles so that someone else—maybe a producer, whom I didn't even know—wouldn't consider me "too intellectual." I vowed: never again. To conceal your standards is to debase them.

Too much of the book publishing business is based on the instinct of going for mass appeal. But this is often done in a manner unsupported by research, numbers, or, not infrequently, taste. I have known various publishers who insisted that flap or back-cover copy on books must be short. The reasoning is that the public has a short attention span. No research has ever supported this among book buyers, who are, in many regards, the self-selected segment of our society that demonstrates a robust attention span. One morning after a meeting in which a publisher insisted on the benefits of short copy I visited a large bookstore and looked at every current bestseller, fiction and nonfiction, hardcover and paperback. I found no correlation between sales and length of jacket copy.

The fulcrum is not whether copy is long or short. It is whether it displays quality. Is the copy specific, clear, and useful? If so, length is irrelevant beyond the physical dimensions of the book. Quality, not brevity, is what matters. I later read this passage in David Ogilvy's indispensable *Ogilvy on Advertising*: "Direct-response advertisers *know* that short copy doesn't sell. In split-run tests, long copy invariably outsells short copy . . . Long copy sells more than short copy, particularly when you are asking the reader to spend a lot of money. Only amateurs use short copy." Allowing for generational language, Ogilvy wrote the immortal line: "The consumer is not a moron, she is your wife."

The same holds true with titles. A good title is basic and clear—or bold and audacious. Audacity must be backed by proof. A production editor once pushed to add the word "secret" to one of my subtitles. I refused. It isn't because I am primly averse to such terms—that word appears in the subtitle to this book. I see a "secret" not so much as something purposefully concealed but as neglected or under-acknowledged and, hence, unseen. I hope I have lived up to the word's use in this book. But I would never employ that term, or any, to attempt low-grade sensationalism.

Some people think a snappy adjective will spice up a title and make a book or movie more commercial. Again, they are wrong. When used randomly or as prov-ocation, adjectives are unsupported claims. They make a statement look weaker rather than stronger. I learned that from years of trial and error as a writer. Without experience, the drive-by editor or keyboard critic rarely understands such language points. Impulse without experience is a poor guide. Verify things for yourself.

I must concede that a lot of what is fleetingly popu-lar online and on social media is steeped in the kinds of cheap language that I am discouraging. But with a price. It may seem harmless to post a snarky comment on social media; but a steady diet of such things numbs us to the anger-inducing properties of perpetual sar-casm and cynicism. Along with this anger comes an absence of empathy and, as alluded earlier, complexity of thought.

Human nature has not changed in the digital era. But the removal of sensory contact and the appearance of anonymity has disinhibited people to let fly their ugliest reactions. I know people personally who display radically different personas online. The online persona is sometimes shallow, curt, and even cruel while in person the individual can be accommodating. I don't believe that leading that kind of double life is powerful; it leads to underdeveloped personas in both worlds.

The clash between tactile and online worlds can be shattering. If you use obnoxious or confrontational tones online it will eventually explode in your face. People lose jobs and reputations, sometimes unfairly, because of one impertinent or poorly timed comment. A TV host for a news network responded emotionally on Twitter during a political feud. This is common, since politics, like money, is highly emotional. The host used a mild profanity. The network fired him. They were probably looking for an excuse to cut him loose over ratings, and also to offer a sacrificial lamb in case they needed to fire someone from the opposite political polarity. He unintentionally handed it to them. Do not be that person. Many of us mix personal lives, business, and politics online. I do myself. It is a combustible mixture. Treat it with care.

I discourage anonymity online. In certain cases, such as for whistleblowers, anonymity is purposeful and necessary. But in many cases I think it's a device for consequence-free cruelty. In an age in which online misinformation and trolling abounds, I think that online interlocutors should receive some kind of "blue check" if they use their real, verified names. I suggest that you not only use your real name but also interact only with people who do, at least in matters of politics or other heated issues. And bear in mind: anonymity is an illusion. If someone wants to find out who's behind a social media account, and they want to badly enough, they usually can.

A good way to start strengthening your speech is to avoid superfluous or gratuitous remarks on social media. I actively use Twitter, Facebook, and Instagram, and I find them excellent tools for staying in touch with readers and announcing projects. I notice, however, that a lot of people comment or complain unnecessarily on social media about a movie, a political figure, or another person's post. I am not suggesting that none of this occur. Sometimes it is funny and revealing. But taken past a certain point these things become blather. I sometimes post political comments, which polarize people even when judiciously worded. But I try to do so with care—there is almost always someone else who can make the same political point I am. I ask myself: is this necessary?

I virtually never block anyone on social media and all my comments are public. But I do occasionally unfriend or unfollow people. My reasons are specific and simple: First, if your aim is to insult or humiliate a private person, or just kick up dust, you're out. Second, if I virtually never hear from someone *except* when they fulminate over a political post, or if they communicate in a vituperative manner, I make room for someone else on the page. I do not have an "anything goes" policy online. I try to provide a constructive tone and expect it in return.

Given the speed and irreversibility of digital media, you must anticipate that some number of your sensitive emails and texts will get read by the wrong people— sometimes the same person about whom you're writing. I've experienced my phone getting hacked and my texts getting read. I didn't write anything I wouldn't stand by, and I didn't use extreme language; but it was jarring and intrusive. You've probably had the experience of someone unintended seeing one or more of your emails, maybe someone on a chain who you meant to exclude and were writing about. I know at least two people who lost their jobs that way, in each case unfairly.

Indeed, when someone unintended sees your email it will *probably* be someone who is mentioned in the communication. Chains and forwarding are widely practiced among various parties to an issue, making the parties themselves likely to be referenced. Hence, the person about whom you may have been commenting is the likeliest uninvited party to your message. Once a television producer made a mildly snarky comment about a member of my management team. He unintentionally included me on the chain. It wasn't too bad and we all took it in stride. But you can only imagination the potential fallout. Another true story: years ago I paused before hitting "send" on a professional email; something made me stop and remove an unnecessary reference to someone being "crazy." I then hit send only to discover that the object of my deletion was *on the chain*. I felt like I was given a governor's reprieve and vowed never to forget it.

A publishing executive once told her staff that you should never put anything in an email that you wouldn't want read aloud in a court of law with you sitting on the witness stand. It's a good rule. It doesn't mean being timorous, but rather using dignified language and reserving sensitive communication for the phone or face to face. It will probably make your message clearer anyway.

*   *   *

I want to close this chapter on a personal note. Since the publication of my 2018 book *The Miracle Club* I have personally experienced divorce. Among the lessons that I learned is that it is greatly important to pay attention, day-by-day and hour-by-hour, to the small needs and comforts of the other person, including what you say. Or don't say.

If you place your spouse first in seemingly small needs you go a long way toward maintaining happiness in your marriage. That is one piece of advice that I would give to every couple. Too often we place our creature comforts—food choices, vacation spots, settings on an alarm, household temperature, the time of meals—before those of the other person. This slowly erodes goodwill and faith. Each of us can make the daily effort to concede such things to a partner. The dividends are more cumulative than they appear.

HABIT 6

GET AWAY FROM CRUEL PEOPLE

People who cut off your air supply must be dismissed.

At the risk of sounding heavy, I believe that too much has been made of forgiveness and acceptance within our spiritual culture. Often it is vital, first and foremost, to physically separate from cruel or depleting people. No amount of self-acceptance or acceptance of others will build immunity to a relative, parent, boss, coworker, or "friend" who makes sport of running you down or who chronically directs passive-aggressive barbs at you.

Hostility is a widespread and under-acknowledged fact of human nature. More important than analyzing or understanding hostility is *getting away from it.* You cannot survive sustained hostility, and should not be expected to. This is true inasmuch as a houseplant cannot survive absence of sunlight or water. Such conditions are unnatural and unnecessary. Questions of forgiveness, understanding, and acceptance, whether of self or another, can be explored *after* you've gotten to safety and protected yourself and your psyche.

In 1945, Napoleon Hill wrote:

> One must remove himself from the range of influence of every person and every circumstance which has even a slight tendency to cause him to feel inferior or incapable of attaining the object of his purpose. Positive egos do not grow in negative environments. On this point there can be no excuse for a compromise, and failure to observe it will prove fatal to the chance of success.

Some people feel unable to separate from a cruel person due to familial ties or financial needs. I sympathize with that—and offer this three-part formula:

1. Be certain that the bonds you feel are actual and not artificial. Fear of disapproval is not a valid excuse for remaining in proximity to a cruel person. Just because someone will disapprove of your decision

to separate is not a real bind. Every decision carries consequences; the positive consequences of distancing from cruelty almost invariably outweigh the negative. Another person's judgment must not deter you. If it does, that is self-created.

2. If you've determined that you authentically wish to separate but feel financially or otherwise bound, vow first to separate from the person internally. Acknowledge to yourself their cruelty and admit its grotesque and destructive nature. Do not tell the other person what you are doing or thinking. Do not share your insight. *Cruel people always have plausible denial.* It is part of how they maintain their hold on you. Just knowing this makes you more powerful.

3. Vow to separate from the offender as a physical fact at the soonest possible opportunity. This opportunity will come, and probably sooner than you think. This is because Cosmic Habit Force, to which I refer in the introduction, sustains and fortifies growth. When you place yourself within its schema, which these steps are designed to do, opportunities for expansion and movement reach and help carry you. But the first and crucial step is determining that this is want you want.

*   *   *

I consider abolitionist hero Frederick Douglass (1818–1895) a voice of universal moral relevance. I want to recount a story from his life, which holds a critical lesson for people of every era and situation, even as it must also be preserved and understood within its historical context.

Born a slave in Maryland around 1818, Douglass was separated as a young child from his mother—a woman who walked miles from another plantation for the rare occasion of rocking him to sleep or giving him a handmade ginger cake. Douglass grew to be a self-educated teenager with an eye on escaping to the north and a determination not to accept the role of complacency to a cruel overseer. But in January 1834, on the eve of his sixteenth birthday, Douglass found himself delivered into the hands of the worst of them, Edward Covey—known locally as "the breaker of Negroes."

A few years earlier, Douglass had been a domestic servant in Baltimore. There the burdens of slavery—the hunger, the beatings, the daily humiliations—were tempered by the surface civilities of city life. The wife of his Baltimore household briefly taught him to read, until her husband abruptly ended the lessons. But Douglass discovered ways to keep building his literacy through whatever books or newspaper scraps could be found. Soon the Baltimore family rearranged its home, and Douglass was returned to plantation life.

His new master in St. Michaels, Maryland, was suspicious: Could a teen who had tasted city life still work the fields? To be brutally certain, at the start of 1834 he "loaned out" Douglass for a year to Covey, a petty, cruel farmer who used every opportunity to beat his new charge on trumped-up offenses. The beatings became so severe that by August Douglass snuck back to his St. Michaels master to beg for protection. The youth, still bruised and caked with blood, was turned away to return to Covey's farm. Once there, Douglass hid all day and into the night in the woods outside Covey's fields, not knowing what to do.

To the shock of Covey, Douglass did return to the farm.* And when beatings resumed, the youth stood up and fought back. For two hours one morning the men struggled, and Covey could not get the better of him. Embarrassed by his inability to control a teenager who had finally said enough, the slave master was forced to back down. For Douglass, it was a moment of inner revolution from which he would never retreat. His act of self-defense, he wrote, had freed him in mind and spirit,

---

* I recount the full episode in *Occult America* (2009), where I focus on the role of the African-American magical tradition of hoodoo.

leaving him to wait for the opportunity when he would finally be free in body.

Even though Douglass writing in three memoirs identified his resistance to Covey as the turning point of his life, it is important to note that he actually did not escape for more than four years. He made plans and was caught in 1836 and finally succeeded in September of 1838 in fleeing from Baltimore to New York City. But Douglass wrote that he was free in spirit the morning he asserted his own sense of personhood. I would never foolishly over-extrapolate from the story of a brutalized and enslaved person to the experience of most of us reading these words today. That would be a grotesque misappropriation. At the same time, a universal moral narrative appears in Douglass's account, and I see him, in addition to being an abolitionist and memoirist, as an ethicist and philosopher. If you've read carefully, you will detect my effort to encapsulate something of his narrative's lessons in the three points upon which I began this chapter.

As alluded in the first of those three points, it is only fair to note that the consequences of separation may be greater than you want to bear. My purpose is to affirm that the *decision is yours alone.* In that vein, I want to describe how I once advised a neighbor and family friend.

In 2012, Hurricane Sandy rocked New York City and many people lost power for days or weeks. A friend, whom I'll call Carol, was stuck in a high-rise building with a young son who was suffering from a fever. She had no power, no elevator service, and couldn't leave the boy alone. Her husband was out of town. She made arrangements to take the boy and stay with her mother-in-law and father-in-law, who lived in a luxury high-rise on Long Island. They had full power. It seemed like a perfect and necessary solution.

But as Carol told it—she's a mature person whose account I take seriously—her mother-in-law, with whom she'd had problems previously, was cruelly unwelcoming. At every turn, the woman made Carol and her recuperating son feel unwelcome and intruding, even though Carol did her best to be a thoughtful guest. At one point Carol told her mother-in-law to please try and understand how difficult this situation was and how she needed a pinch of tolerance. "Well, this is no picnic for me either," was the woman's abrupt response.

Carol was deeply hurt by the experience. She recalled other times when her in-law had acted slighting or hostile. She was understandably upset. No stranger to therapy, spirituality, or self-help, she had tried for years to navigate and leaven the situation, but to no avail.

I told her: "Carol, have you considered that you could simply separate from this person? If her behavior is perpetually hostile, you could simply say no to holidays and other contacts. There may be consequences, but there are already consequences—you're in pain. Why be around her?"

She explained that she wanted her son to be raised within a family circle, and to have adults who could serve as role models or sources of dependability. I noted that her mother-in-law was neither of those things, and her son already had lots of positive adults in his life.

I could see that she was energized by the notion that *there is an option*. I didn't feel that it was my business to push the point further and I don't think the separation ever occurred. But I wanted my friend to realize a broadened sense of possibility. It is powerful simply to know that *the choice is in your hands*, and can always be renewed or revisited however you go. *You do not have to be around cruel people.*

Once you decide to separate from cruelty, you'll be amazed at how many other facets of your life improve. In many cases, you will rediscover yourself as a person of humor, even-temper, reliability, and steadiness. I have been astonished to observe how many problems that get attributed to character, trauma, dysfunction, or over-sensitivity (a charge that cruel people almost always use to control you) suddenly lift once you are in the right company.

I believe that our therapeutic culture—positive as it has been in many ways—has inculcated many of us with the myth that our problems perpetually follow us unless we resolve the psychological root causes. That is true in some cases. But in many cases I believe that children and adults are simply and egregiously misplaced. They are in the wrong kinds of company where they may feel bullied, misunderstood, or disdained. An altered setting can work dramatic changes both personally and professionally.

I have been in settings where I had neighbors who were inconsiderate or hostile. Where my every effort at rapprochement ended disappointingly. I used to own a lake house in Upstate New York. When I drove up and saw my neighbor's car in his driveway my stomach would tighten—and this was a place for relaxation!—because he perpetually encroached on our property with noise, fireworks, spotlights, crowds, and a not infrequent wisecrack. No effort, from spiritual affirmations to a high fence, made much difference. When I finally moved I felt great. I had been in the wrong setting. I am mindful that moving or breaking ties is not always possible. I owned that house for fifteen years. But I want you to understand that sometimes the only solution is in using your feet.

HABIT 7
CHOOSE YOUR COMRADES

The individual is plural.

The March 2020 issue of *Vogue* dedicated an extensive spread to pop star Billie Eilish. The magazine anointed the singer-songwriter as both the reflection and the driver of a significant segment of youth culture. *Vogue*'s lavishly illustrated piece, featuring captivating images of Eilish by a variety of fashion photographers and a piece of stunning fan art from Russia, explored the teen's experience with depression and alienation, and her psychological connection with young fans.

It is impossible not to admire Eilish, whose unstudied elegance and vulnerability make her a figure from whom you cannot easily look away. But as I read the *Vogue* piece I had to keep reminding myself that this person just turned eighteen. At the time of this writing we hang on her utterances, but she is just out of childhood. The allure of Eilish is partly amalgamation. I don't mean that in a negative way. Her music reveals an extraordinary and expressive voice, subtle lyrics, and a distinct tech-minimalist sound. But the star is, for better or worse, an assemblage of everyone around her, including parents, managers, producers, interviewers, photographers, and *Vogue* writers and editors.

This is, in various ways, true of all of us. This is true not only in our commercial or working lives, but in our ethical, intimate, and creative lives as well. Hence, the inspiration for the title of his chapter: Choose Your Comrades. Your most critical decision in life, observed twentieth-century Italian novelist Ignacio Silone (1900–1978), is "the choice of comrades."

For years I attempted to break through as a television host and writer, shooting pitch reel after pitch reel with production companies where I had few friends, affinities, or dedicated collaborators. Hard as I worked, the final product was always so-so. But in late 2018, I met a team of producers and a director and screenwriter, Jacqueline Castel, who I felt elevated everything that they worked on. Entering into the flow of work with these people changed the creative atmosphere for me. They include manager Lalo Barrón, producer Sean Huntley, photographer Larry Busacca, and filmmaker Ronni Thomas. These changes have touched not only my work life but also my personal relationships.

In the previous chapter I talked about the consequences of living in the wrong neighborhood, literally or figuratively. That kind of situation leaves you constantly questioning yourself. People take you down in ways that you are too slow to anticipate or respond to. You put up with subpar or disrespectful behavior. Never blame yourself for this—it is a universal human problem. For one thing, our intellects run slower than our emotions. Hence we can feel flummoxed and outmatched when faced with aggression, both subtle and direct. This is all the more reason to self-determine your environment.

Years ago on a television talk show the activist and social critic Michelangelo Signorile responded to a young caller who said that as a gay youth he was tormented in his small town, which had a strong fundamentalist streak. Signorile told him, and I paraphrase, "You're terrific and there's nothing wrong with you—don't listen to the crazies. At the soonest possible opportunity move to the first large or medium-sized city you can find and build your own life."

I applaud his response for more reasons than may be apparent. I believe we get roped into spending inordinate amounts of time and energy engaged in chronic (and often depleting) reflection and self-analysis, when often what is truly needed is a change of venue and "choice of comrades."

When I moved from Queens to Long Island as a young adolescent I encountered an environment that was conformist and oppressive. The act of taking a single step outside the norm, in music, body adornment, or any kind of self-expression, was met with contempt. I kept thinking that *I* needed fixing. When I returned to New York City as a young adult those feelings significantly abated. Whenever they resurface today, I find that I am usually in the wrong company. Locating the right company is a matter of following your affinities. That sounds simple but so much disrupts it. One of the barriers we face is that we sometimes deflect the *very thing we profess to want*, to which I now turn.

Philosophers have long observed that we bring about our worst fears. In the Greek myth of Oedipus, the king is prophesied to murder his father and wed his mother. He is so fearful of his fate that by rash actions he actualizes the prophecy and exposes his crime. Oedipus is one of the core parables of human nature. Over and over, we can observe how people produce their worst fears, pushing away support systems and pursuing destructive behaviors. Although we can analyze *how* this occurs it is not always easy to understand *why* it occurs—and does so with fearful symmetry.

I haven't cracked the riddle of Oedipus. But I have observed the manner in which people inadvertently deflect relationships that they desire, or say they do. Primarily, this occurs through *over-compensation* of one's perceived flaws or deficiencies. For example, a person is sometimes so eager to gain entry to a peer group that he forces himself on others to the extent of rendering himself unappealing or irritating. This may occur by interrupting conversations, steering conversations back to himself, making unwanted criticism or commentary—doing things to render himself noticeable while actually inviting disdain. In a related phenomenon, some people seek *negative attention*, unconsciously (and unsuccessfully) soliciting help or sympathy by advertising their most distorted traits.

Over-compensation is your worst ally when pursuing desirable company.

When seeking the right company look carefully at whom you wish to be among and pick up on their signals—in speech, cadence, interests, humor, values, and sympathies. Be sure they are the company that you really want. Lowering your standards or artificially altering them is not only unappealing but also makes you dishonest. One of my heroes was literary critic and democratic socialist Irving Howe, who died in 1993. I learned a lot from him, although he had no interest in the spiritual topics to which I later dedicated myself. After his memorial service, a contemporary of his approached me, grabbed my hand, and said: "Mitch—*standards*. If you want to learn one thing from Irving, it is standards." I never forgot it. You should possess a baseline of personal and professional standards that are non-negotiable. Learn if others share them, not to judge them but to discover true sympathies. If you come to admire someone, do not be afraid to express it. Too many people think being cool means being aloof. It means being self-determined. Never hide your standards. Or be afraid to show enthusiasm when someone meets or surpasses them.

Above all, never settle for low company. I have felt the sting of loneliness and I can say with absolute sympathy: *It is vastly better to be nobly alone than debased with unfit friends.* This is true for adolescents, too. You are far more likely to attract the right kinds of friends or love interests by accepting a noble aloneness and waiting until the necessary people enter your sightline. I know how difficult it is to follow that counsel—and I know how rich its rewards are.

Any mate or romantic partner who makes you struggle to feel valued or respected should be cut off. Even with the best "strategy," you will never get what you want, you will only drag out your loss. If you find yourself obsessively consulting with friends (or a Tarot deck) to decipher your mate's behavior, to plan your next move, to unravel his or her signals, the odds are that you are in an ill-fitting relationship. The Talmud warns against fraternizing with people who make inscrutable or clever remarks to imply a covert meaning. All the more important to beware of intimates who reverse, conceal, or confuse you with their motives.

You will experience a vastly greater sense of self and be more attractive to others—as well as get on with the task of finding the right relationship—by severing ties when a partner doesn't overtly value you. Strategy doesn't build a relationship. Strategizing in a love relationship reminds me of a paraphrased expression from Prussian Field Marshal Helmuth von Moltke (1800–1891): "Every plan immediately fails upon contact with the enemy."

I was once seeing someone who had ambivalent feelings about our relationship. She wanted to see other people. I did not. One day while I was under a strict writing deadline she called me with this proposition, which she obviously felt strongly about. The timing was odd since we had just spent some very satisfying time together and she had showered me with loving messages. I thought, "We want different things and I'm getting a signal that I should end this, or at least take a break."

I spoke with my shrink and a close friend. Both advised me to cool out and not take any steps. I cooled out. Later I decided that I would accede to her proposal and we'd see others. Soon after, the same person sent me a shockingly brusque text breaking up with me. (Yes—a breakup text between adults.) Although painful, it was for the best since I met someone with whom I was vastly more simpatico.

Even though my shrink and my friend had wanted the best for me, my first instinct was right: this relationship was headed nowhere. You've felt this, too—and you've been right. Any romantic relationship punctuated by suffering or confusion is in a slow-motion death spiral. I've never seen an exception. In matters of dating and romance, people often subject themselves to fruitless torment, believing that ashes can be revived into a fire or that they'll rue the loss of their lover. Better to act with decisiveness. Morbid obsession, strategizing, and consultations with friends are no substitute for the togetherness you seek. If anything, they deter it.

Of course, you must ask yourself what you really desire in friends, collaborators, and partners. Sometimes we tell ourselves we want something that we do not. I've seen friends profess to want a steady romantic partner but continually date erratic or immature people, guaranteeing a story to tell over wine but deferring any kind of meaningful relationship. I ask myself if they really want to be with someone; or if they want drama and friction. Or even solitude, which is a fine choice.

We rarely question our behavioral patterns and the results they bring, as though repetition reflects what we really want. Repetition is misleading. The repetitive act may satisfy something *other than* what you claim to want. If you see someone chronically provoking or arguing with family, friends, or a spouse (or maybe with you), it is likely that the thrill of argument is exactly what he is seeking. That will never be acknowledged. It needn't be. But just ask yourself: "What is being accomplished?" The effect usually reveals the motive. This is especially true for patterned behavior. I had a family member who would constantly, without prompt or provocation, pull a grenade pin, saying or doing things that could only produce conflict and hurt feelings. No great complexity was at work. No web of psychological subtleties. People simply enjoy conflict and contest, even when it's self-destructive. Be sure this isn't you. And sever ties with those who act this way.

"There is one very important point about being happy," Joseph Murphy wrote in 1963. "You must sincerely desire to be happy." That may seem like an obtuse assertion. Don't we all *want* happiness? Take a second look. Negative emotions are addictive. They bring a strange thrill. Like riding a rollercoaster or watching a horror movie. They bring attention, albeit of a negative sort. This is why the role of victim or bully is closely related, or even one and the same. Before you can attain happiness you must be certain that you truly *want* it. Don't rely on assumption. Search your psyche and your behaviors.

Part of choosing the right comrades means knowing how to maintain relationships. Chemistry is rare—preserve it.

Several years before his death in 2002, musician Joe Strummer, cofounder of The Clash—a group that meant everything to me (and still does)—reflected on the band's dissolution in the early 1980s:

Whatever a group is, it is the chemical mixture of those four people that makes a group work. That's a lesson everyone should learn: you don't mess with it. If it works, just let it . . . do whatever you have to do to bring it forward, but don't mess with it. We learned that bitterly.

*   *   *

When you a have productive partnership don't assume it can be replicated. It is worth preserving through periods of friction, which are inevitable. At some point it may be necessary to let a collaborative partnership go. But do so carefully. Make sure that positive things are happening in your life and in your work *that are organically replacing the thing that you're releasing.*

My observation is that rather than assume new things will come, allow their unfoldment to play out first or at least sprout. Thereafter you can loosen or sever old bonds of commerce and collaboration. Once a fruitful bond is broken it cannot be reestablished. So never approach collaborative breakups rashly. Of course, what I am prescribing pertains only to *productive* relations—not partnerships that are glued together by fear of change, which are always worth losing.

HABIT 8

SPEND FOR POWER

---

*Spend only on what builds
your ability to earn.*

No issue other than sex is more confounding and emotional than money. Everyone wants more of it. Everyone has a complex relationship to it. I am no financial wizard. But I am a full-time artist (and ex-publishing executive) who co-supports two children, pays for his own healthcare (don't get me started), and manages his finances gainfully and responsibly. I can share what I believe in and what I've discovered.

First it must be said that money well spent and well saved is *power*. There is no questioning that. Money commands respect, attention, fear, service, and privilege. It may not buy you love, but it buys access to beautiful surroundings, education, art, influence, health (under certain circumstances), and even eroticism. It funds projects. It paid for this book you're reading. It is a medium of agency, force, and politics. Next to sexuality, it possesses limitless allure. Set aside all Pollyannaish attitudes about money. People who claim not to care about money often have hidden access to it through family ties, spouses, or other means. We *all* care about it.

For years I denied my vital connection to money. I was too slow or timorous in asking for right compensation, and in asking for it in a timely, responsible, and transparent manner. This approach held down my income.

"I believe most people are inadequately compensated," Joseph Murphy wrote in *The Power of Your Subconscious Mind*. "One of the causes many people do not have more money is that they are silently or openly condemning it." I take this statement seriously—I observed this attitude in myself. For many years I considered money secondary in my publishing career, and I probably considered it a mark of compromise. As a result, I spent years being under-compensated.

I accepted without any real questioning or negotiating the standard yearly raises that were handed out in the publishing business where I was employed for nearly thirty years. Belatedly in my career I finally determined to require compensation that reflected the billing I was bringing into my company. In early 2012, I wrote a memo that plainly laid out the profit margins of the books I published, as well as various ways I was strengthening my imprint's bottom line. (One of my proudest accomplishments was that no one got laid off while I was editor-in-chief during and after the 2008 recession, which drove the book chain Borders out of business and shrank profits across the industry.) I named a specific salary and title that I wanted, and I got it. After many years, I had reversed my inadequate assessment of my own contributions. In so doing, I shed a fearful if not negative attitude toward money.

Carefully scan your attitude toward money. Like relationships, we sometimes harbor deep-seated conflicts toward money without examining or even being aware of them. You owe it to yourself to determine whether any aspect of your outlook is detracting from your financial success.

A related problem with money reemerged as I settled into my livelihood as a fulltime writer and speaker in late 2017. When asked to deliver a talk or write an article I often said yes too quickly. Sometimes I agreed in principle before the financial and logistical questions were fully resolved. I spent too little time scrutinizing exactly what was being offered, not only in terms of money but also in matters of timing, payout, rights, and creative control. When writing an article, I didn't discuss its placement, such as being featured on the cover. I gave too many quick "yeses" out of fear. Eager to build my career and ensure that I could make a living at it, I sometimes agreed impulsively.

This was a misapplication of the principle of expeditiousness, which we explore more fully in the following chapter. I was not acting with decisiveness; I was acting from the opposite. I said yes so quickly that I sometimes found myself working with feckless or low-energy people. I said yes to offers that paid too little. It was only in late 2019 that I began to dramatically shed those habits, which, in varying ways, had held sway for years.

When you receive an offer for a project you must approach it with a balance of enthusiasm and scrutiny. *Never disrespect an offer.* It is disrespectful not to acknowledge its receipt in a timely way. If someone emails you an offer, acknowledge it immediately even if you need time to consider it. I once emailed an offer to a writer who failed to acknowledge it even after I followed up. At the end of the day I withdrew it. At that very moment (surprise!) I heard back from him with some strange excuse. I reinstated the offer and made the deal. He never delivered an acceptable book, or cooperated in any meaningful way. People who do not respect offers cannot be trusted to respect any aspect of their work relationships.

At the same time, offers should be carefully vetted. If you feel there is room for improvement or negotiation always make the ask. If done respectfully, the other party will, or should, come back to you with some accommodation or explanation. Perhaps I'm biased but, generally speaking, the boilerplate terms offered by most publishing houses are usually sound because publishing contracts in the U.S. are fairly standard and are the cumulative project of longstanding industry negotiations. During my years at Penguin Random House I was proud of the transparency of our agreements. Hence, in literary work, I do not believe that an agent is always necessary, although I acknowledge that your average long-form publishing contract is filled with arcana, much of it rarely pertinent.

There are, of course, times when a quick "yes" is warranted. When you have reason to feel that you are receiving a good offer from an honorable person do not delay. I made many dozens of such offers in my publishing years and I always appreciated a quick answer. It is not naïve to instinctively feel that an offer and a partnership are sound. I don't mean this to contradict what I've just written about scrutiny; this is another area of paradox, which must be respected. Do not be foolishly consistent and withhold an enthusiastic yes when everything lines up.

A lawyer from South Africa once told me that a handshake is worth more than a contract, because all a contract does is mitigate risk. A contract is no augur of a good relationship. Indeed, if you're looking at the contract to manage the relationship, you're already in trouble. A contract can only limit your losses. This lawyer's principle was that your feeling about whether the other party is trustworthy is as valuable, or more so, than a document. An honorable person will pay on time and heed agreements; a piece of paper will never change that for better or worse. I believe in this principle. Although you must be careful not to over-apply it. As a Muslim expression goes, "Trust in Allah but tie your camel." Whether to say yes is a matter of trust; what the yes consists of sometimes must be worked out very carefully.

Once you've agreed on terms, you must then view yourself as being on the same team. When signature is put to paper, unless there is a violation of terms, you must view your collaborators or backers as partners. If you take an oppositional stance after signature, you are going to poison the project. On one occasion I took a newly signed author out to a celebratory lunch; before I had slipped out of my coat as we settled into the booth of an expensive sushi restaurant, he told me: "First of all, I just want to say I don't think I was paid enough for this book." It was not only bad form but it proved an omen: he never delivered an acceptable book and the project was canceled.

The issues that I'm writing about run riot in the New Age world in which I function as a writer, speaker, and former publisher. In alternative and traditional spiritual circles there exist sketchy attitudes and practices around money, something that strikes many people, me included, as a bitter irony. Before I venture into more general financial advice, and assuming many people reading these words have some connection to the worlds of New Age and therapeutic spirituality, I want to make some observations about navigating that landscape.

Many people in the body-mind-spirit field dream of quitting their day job and becoming the next Deepak Chopra, Marianne Williamson, or Tony Robbins. But it's important to consider that, with few exceptions, many New Age "stars" lead a Willy Lomanesque existence of persistent travel, so-so accommodations, and slow or low pay. Some figure out myriad ways to earn money from talks, cruises, conferences, and digital events, in the process selling lots of books and AV programs on deep wholesale discounts. But most of us lack the instincts or, frankly, the desire to do it that way. For one thing, being constantly on the go doesn't leave much time for quality writing.

Most speakers and authors who really break through on the metaphysical circuit discover that headlining a weekend event, which may require hours of travel and workshop commitment, grosses $5,000 or so. Not bad, but not rock star fees. And there lots of logistics involved, sometimes handled by volunteers or staffers who are not exactly top grads from hotel-management school. I have stayed in accommodations with leaky pipes and stains that I won't even speculate over because an event planner didn't make the hotel booking until the day before the gig.

When money is involved, matters turn more serious. I will no longer speak at one prominent New Age center in the northeast because after three events in a row they would not pay me until months of (unreturned) phone calls and emails, resulting, finally, in my contacting the program director who greenlighted the check. When something occurs three times consecutively it's a policy. Musicians and standup comics often speak of getting stiffed or shorted by nightclubs and promoters. I'm sure that strippers and sex workers experience this. Well, unfortunately, it's no different on the New Age circuit. Although you're told namaste while your check is being withheld, which may be worse.

And travel only gets tougher as you age. One well-known prosperity minister used to tour the nation in her advanced years with a large suitcase of books and audio programs to sell at events. Hauling your own wares like a mystical stevedore is an exhausting way of life. But many growth centers and event venues do not order your books; they permit you to sell them there. And sometimes take a cut. Moreover, the types of metaphysical churches at which this prosperity minister spoke often collect "love offerings," which means that your fee, or part of it, is based on congregant contributions. It places the burden on the speaker to rope in audiences.

An increasingly common and viable option that I haven't discussed is running your own online seminars, vlogs, podcasts (a crowded field!), and related digital coaching or consulting. All of that requires great talent and persistence and quality content. It comes with a considerable workload but frees you from much of what I've just described.

If you're working on the body-mind-spirit circuit, and you have your eyes on the grail, take this advice:

- **DON'T BE OVEREAGER TO QUIT YOUR DAY JOB.** Cultivate the excellence of what you do without an immediate eye on platform and audience. Lead with quality.

- **IF ON THE ROAD, BE DEFINITE ABOUT YOUR FEE, PER DIEM, AND TRAVEL REQUIREMENTS.** Make it part of the first stage of your conversation with event planners. Don't worry about frightening venues away; the ones that get frightened away never had the resources to start with.

- **BE WARY OF PRESENTING FOR FREE.** Sometimes it is necessary to provide services free to establish yourself at a venue or build your resume. Be certain, however, that you understand your motives. *Because "free" usually means unvalued.* I once spoke gratis at a fundraiser at a now-closed growth center in New York City and then had to spend weeks chasing down $80 that their bookstore owed me.

- **SAY NO.** It is better for your morale, finances, and blood pressure to speak at three of the right gigs each year than thirty so-so ones. Your energy is not endlessly renewable.

- **DON'T GET HUNG UP ON "BIG BREAKS."** Presenters sometimes agree to events because they think that *one person* may hear them who will broadcast their message or make their career. That almost never happens.

- **DO IT *YOUR* WAY.** There is no single template to success. The thing I love about the earlier generations of metaphysical speakers—people like Neville Goddard, Edgar Cayce, and Florence Scovel Shinn—is that they were self-made, self-published, and had no particular plan, platform, brand, or slogan. Today they are legends.

You can also navigate these issues by having a really solid speaking agent or business manager. I have that person in my life today. But for many years I did not. For much of your career you may not either. It takes a long time to find or attract the right person. In the interim, the best thing you can give to a self-help audience is the example of your own recovery, success, or workaday philosophy of life. Cultivate that first. Then take it bigger—on your own terms.

So much for my advice for Aquarian-Age entrepreneurs. I now want to provide basic financial advice that will serve anyone. In managing money in the broadest sense—particularly in deciding when to make a purchase—I have benefited greatly from Ralph Waldo Emerson's essay "Wealth" published in his 1860 collection *The Conduct of Life*. Part of Emerson's greatness as a writer is that he never shied away from practicality. This was true of his philosophical descendant William James, whom I quote in the introduction. It can be argued that Emerson's most practical works, which include "Wealth," were not among his greatest. In *The American Newness*, critic Irving Howe wrote that in such works the philosopher "merely tugs the complexities . . . into the shallows of the explicit."

I venerate this critic and there is truth to his charge. And yet his judgment does not take full account of Emerson's authorial bravery. Emerson felt obligated to be direct—to provide his readers with *plans of action*. If this approach reduced his philosophical heights, it also banished any prospect of evasion. Emerson would not avoid the question of *how* to practice the kinds of self-driven living that his philosophical essays endorsed. For that reason, his work has been a beacon to me.

In "Wealth," Emerson declares, chin out, that the individual is "born to be rich." By riches, the philosopher is not waxing metaphorical; he means cold, hard cash. But he also identifies accumulation of capital as benefitting only that person who uses it to productive ends. Emerson writes,

> Every man is a consumer, and ought to be a producer.
> He fails to make his place good in the world, unless
> he not only pays his debt, but also adds something

to the common wealth. Nor can he do justice to his genius, without making some larger demand on the world than a bare subsistence. He is by constitution expensive, and needs to be rich.

Only *those purchases that expand your power and abilities*, Emerson argues, leave you any richer. Wealth that fails to abet expansion is wealth thrown away. "Nor is the man enriched," Emerson writes, "in repeating the old experiments of animal sensation." Rather, you are enriched when you increase your ability to earn, to do, to produce, and to grow. Wealth, properly understood, is power. And it must be used toward ends that increase your power.

So, how do you earn wealth? Emerson outlines roughly three steps: 1) First filling some nonnegotiable, subsistence-level need in your own life: this is what drove the primeval farmers, hunter-gatherers, and villagers. 2) Next, applying one's particular talents to nature, and expansively filling the needs of others. If you do not know or understand your talents, you must start there before anything is possible. Your particular talent should be a source of excellence. And, finally, 3) using your wealth for the purposes of productiveness: paying down debts, making compound investments, and procuring the tools and talents of your trade. Building and expanding is the only sound way to riches. And such things also reflect your code and fiber as a progressing being.

Before I make a purchase I always ask myself: Will this build me as a person? Will it enable my aims? That doesn't mean abstaining from entertainment, which is a vital part of recharging and enjoying life with others. (Although even in this area I select entertainment along the lines of self-development or the "augmentive" principle explored in chapter one.) Making purpose-driven purchases does not mean eschewing items that might seem luxurious, like a cherished item of clothing. As I alluded in the chapter on Total Environment, an accessory, accoutrement, or piece of clothing can do wonders for your sense of selfhood, attractiveness, and personal performance. If selected wisely and properly cared for it is an investment. A friend who attended fashion school in Paris told me that her teacher wore the same black Chanel skirt every day to class. At first, my friend thought it was weird. She later realized that the teacher was displaying a principle: it is better to look your best in one truly great item than to rotate various so-so items.

I sometimes fail on the scale of purposeful purchases. I dine out too often. I noticed one year that I was spending far too much on rideshare services like Uber. I put an immediate stop to that. I found it easier, cheaper, and healthier to bike more of the time. I was less decisive at reducing meals out, which I find relaxing and primetime for socializing. So there are allowances to be made—but only if you can make them without consuming money for essentials while paying down debt and saving, to which we now turn.

There exist a dizzying number of financial guides on the market, many of them with sparkly, last-guide-you'll-ever-need titles. Among the legion of books that extol financial know-how, I treasure the old standby *The Richest Man In Babylon* by George S. Clason. It is built on a few simple plans and rules, most of which underlie much of today's personal-finance wizardry. I consider the book's lessons as sturdy as when the author first started expounding on them in 1926.

"Pay yourself first" is the central (and often copied) lesson of Clason's guide, which he presents as a series of fictional parables from the Mesopotamian empire. Clason meant that you must set aside at least ten-percent of your earnings in savings—now a standard principle in financial guides—and dedicate the remainder of your money to reducing debt, procuring a home or other investment properties, buying insurance, caring for your family, and only then allowing yourself to spend on life's pleasures.

Clason's approach is one of enlightened thrift. "Every piece of gold you save is a slave to work for you," one of his ancient characters says. Clason wants the reader to see that abstaining from spending is not a dreary act but a powerful one, since the dollar you save is invested or used to erase interest-bearing debt. He does not endorse asceticism; he wants money management approached in a spirit of adventure—knowing that your prudence will pay off in comfort and security. This is the aim of his lessons to thrift and safe investment. And he got rich himself offering them.

In the early-twentieth century, Clason was a Denver-based publisher of maps and atlases. He published the first road atlas of the United States and Canada. In 1926, he hit upon an idea that later saved his own finances and preserved his name as one of the most practical self-help writers of the last century. Clason began writing his series of pamphlets on managing personal finances, which banks, insurance companies, and brokerage houses bought in bulk and distributed free to their clients. The mapmaker's pamphlets proved so popular that in 1930 he grouped them together in a single volume, *The Richest Man in Babylon*, which he issued from his own publishing company. Clason Publishing did not survive the Great Depression. But *The Richest Man in Babylon* did—and in the years ahead it emerged as a mainstay of popular financial literature.

Clason's outlook was always ardently business-friendly, which fueled its popularity in establishment circles. Companies that sold insurance, issued home loans, or maintained savings accounts had everything to like about his work. Clason endorsed financial products along with a whistle-while-you-work ethic. Che Guevera, he wasn't. But for all his institutional friendliness, Clason proffered principled advice. His book contains not a trite or unrealistic passage.

For me, the book's most effective chapter is "The Camel Trader of Babylon," which is about the imperative of paying down your debts, and the feelings of nobility that accrue to the individual who does so, even if incrementally. This reminds me of a passage that I read as a teen from the Talmudic book *Ethics of the Fathers*: "Who is evil?" a rabbi asks his students. After rumination, the answer comes: "He who borrows and does not repay." That statement must be understood on many levels; but one cannot neglect the material level.

Keep in mind that debts mean not only monetary borrowings, but also deadlines or obligations in any area of life where you've given your word. If you've vowed to complete a task, even a seemingly small domestic chore, or to show up at a certain time, then do so. You'd be surprised how carefully people note such things, including your financial partners, customers, clients, and backers. Regardless of how you see yourself, you are evaluated and defined by your incremental workaday ethics. Whether or not you are aware of it, you also experience your own inner sense of personal performance and reliability; this can feed feelings of anger and defensiveness, or of dignity and rightness.

It is, of course, natural to give yourself a pass for times when you feel justifiably late or in default on a financial commitment: aren't there exceptions for unforeseen circumstance? Yes; but you should always be very disciplined about such cases. As a friend once put it: "The only real emergency is a medical emergency." Consider this before you defer a debt, a domestic project, or a commitment to pay someone, like a contractor, vendor, or artist.

Indeed, I believe there is a special ethic in paying people quickly, especially artists, contractors, and independently employed people who have no source of income other than their fees-for-service. If you delay paying such people, or if you are slow in responding to their queries, you should pause to imagine your own paycheck or direct deposit not arriving, and your getting no immediate reply from your boss, payroll manager, or HR department. How would you feel? That's what independent contractors routinely experience.

It should be kept in mind that paying someone quickly and reliably is *free*. It doesn't increase your out-of-pocket obligations. But what you purchase in good will or loyalty is immeasurable. For me, the dividing line between venues for which I will no longer work, and publishers and venues for which I will move mountains is accountability and expeditiousness with regard to paying. It says more than the payer knows.

Clason helped clarify another principle for me: *You should dedicate twice as much money to your debts as to your savings.* Immediately save your ten percent; but twenty percent should go toward debt. Debt is intrinsically a drain both in terms of interest and reputation (as well as credit score). If you have the liquidity, erase your debt entirely, especially credit card debt. But if you do not have the cash flow, then make every effort to pay it down at double the rate of your savings, while neglecting neither.

Sometimes people's debts are greater than their income. Even during such periods, endeavor to follow these rules just the same. Even if you know you will be dipping into your savings to pay a bill, or (more likely) adding to your credit-card balance, do not neglect to apply these percentages. Do this even while debts are growing. The reason is that it makes this modest plan into a steady habit, so that when you are eventually able to regain solvency you have a sound set of financial principles your back.

Given that I am completing these words during the coronavirus pandemic, which is shaking the finances of nearly every household, I must add a special caveat. During periods of financial crisis it is vital to maintain liquidity. In such cases it is advisable to cease paying down debt (other than managing legally minimum payments) in order to sustain your cash on hand. This is a general rule only during periods of true crisis.

A final word for freelancers and the self-employed. In addition to everything that I have outlined, you must take 30% off the top of your gross receipts and set it aside in a firewalled savings account for taxes. Do this even if you pay your estimated federal taxes quarterly. Pay it from that account. You'll breath a huge sigh of relief down the road. Maintain this practice always.

None of what I've written has yet addressed health insurance, prescriptions, or medical costs. Those things are financial barriers that were far less known in Clason's era. Healthcare and health insurance present a grave financial difficulty, and often impossibility, for millions of Americans as I write these words in early 2020. Political reforms may eventually control pharmaceutical prices, create an affordable health-insurance option, and protect consumers dealing with recalcitrant and misleading insurance companies. These things are a national crisis. Until reform arrives—and I hope it does soon apropos of when I'm writing these words— my operative principle is that most health insurance in America today is organized crime with a refrigerator magnet. Hence, their "services"—which are based on a model of taking in as high a premium as possible and paying out as few claims as possible—must be approached with prudential thought and caution.

If you work in a corporate or union job and receive good health insurance you are fortunate. Yet even those plans have considerable gaps and lock you into a group model where you have very little consumer choice. If you are an independent worker, service worker, or contractor, the options become thinner and more stressful. Most personal finance writers ignore or gloss over this reality in their programs to wealth and solvency.

For example, in 2020 a personal finance writer at Medium wrote an article about a Vermont janitor who died with $8 million in the bank, which he left to his local library and hospital. It sounds like a great American parable: the "millionaire next door" makes good through savings and thrift, and it's all the more touching that the self-made philanthropist was a laborer. But this article and others about the wealthy janitor, including pieces at CNBC, omitted one crucial fact. The man served in World War II—and there's the answer: *he had lifelong healthcare through the Veterans Administration.* That's what made it all possible. I know a cat sitter in Manhattan who has amassed a huge portfolio through his Roth IRA. He's a wonderful eccentric who lives cheaply in a rent-controlled apartment, eschews digital culture, cable, cell service, eating out, and most luxuries. He exists like an urban Thoreau. Like the janitor, he's also a millionaire. And like his counterpart, he is a veteran, in this case from Vietnam. He receives lifelong VA coverage, which got him through a harrowing illness.

If these thrifty men didn't have VA coverage, all of the money that they wisely invested would've been wiped out by a single health disaster, chronic condition, or purchasing of their own insurance. It is that simple. Few people who write on investment strategies or personal finance get it. We need more working people in financial journalism who know what it means to purchase insurance or otherwise cover health costs without a corporate or family net.

I wish I had a magic bullet to offer in this area, but I do not. If you have children then you need insurance; it's that simple. The night before writing these words I watched a working mother close out her shift at a Starbucks at 9:30 p.m. with her two young kids in the store. I'm sure it was against company policy to have the kids there—and I applaud her coworkers for supporting her. She probably holds the job because she needs the company's insurance. I once knew a pregnant woman who suffered terrible burns and would've been left without coverage but for a sympathetic and heroic administrator at the VA who shifted around some dates and arranged for her to remain on her veteran father's coverage. I've watched pharmacists give away meds for free to people who couldn't afford them. These are flukes that people cling to for life in a nation where for-profit and unregulated health insurance has become a rolling catastrophe.

If you're single, you can consider eschewing health insurance. Most of the Affordable Care Act plans that are anywhere near affordable are limited in coverage, do not include prescriptions, and come with high deductibles. You might consider whether they are worth it at all. I wish there existed catastrophic-care plans that really held down costs and allowed you to plan for emergencies, but those are difficult to find especially if you're over 40. Earlier I said that health insurance is organized crime with a refrigerator magnet. I was not being cute. The problem that independent consumers face is that most healthcare companies decline some number of legitimate claims, which customers have actually paid for. No one knows how much. They do this through arcane coding procedures. We need transparency laws. It is clear from the testimony of countless people that health insurance companies have erected an abusive and unregulated system of denying coverage: they exploit every scenario to wear down the consumer and reject a fixed portion of valid claims. This is politically scandalous (or ought to be) and morally unconscionable.

All I am really trying to say—and I wish I had better advice for you—is to think twice before purchasing coverage, or to think flexibly about your coverage needs, because the current insurance schema is stacked against the consumer. I feel that I owe you a personal accounting in this regard. I currently pay for my own coverage and I take it month-by-month, uncertain about the ultimate cost-to-benefit ratio. I am, of course, very aware of the inconceivable expense of uninsured medical care, which is why I elect to maintain coverage. As a single person I can make it work. But if I had to purchase insurance for my two adolescent sons (who are covered through my ex-wife's plan) it would be near impossible, although there are certain New York State public options and options in some other states. I write all this because you as the reader deserve transparency, and I will not sell you on a financial scenario that glosses over the crisis of health insurance.

Virtually every technique in this book is applicable whether you have a corporate or an independent job. But in terms of managing health insurance the long-term solution must come through political action and sane public policy. Until reform arrives, I urge you to research the matter carefully, weigh the public and private options, and approach the question with steely-eyed realism. I know many artists who forego coverage. It is not because they are naïve. It is because the system makes it unmanageable.

HABIT 9

NEVER DITHER

Time dissipates energy.

Earlier I quoted from William James's 1895 essay, "Is Life Worth Living?" That and Ralph Waldo Emerson's 1841 essay "Compensation" are probably the closest things I have to a personal creed. James noted that self-belief is not something we engage in for vanity or some abstract need for self-affirmation. Belief in self does not guarantee success, otherwise every self-inflated peacock would succeed. Rather, it is a critical ingredient to the possibility of success. To the *maybe* of success. James wrote:

Not a victory is gained, not a deed of faithfulness or courage is done, except upon a maybe . . . It is only by risking our persons from one hour to another that we live at all. And often enough our faith beforehand in an uncertified result *is the only thing that makes the result come true.* Suppose, for instance, that you are climbing a mountain and have worked yourself into a position from which the only escape is by a terrible leap. Have faith that you can successfully make it, and your feet are nerved to its accomplishment. But mistrust yourself, and think of all the sweet things you have heard the scientists say of maybes, and you will hesitate so that, at last, all unstrung and trembling, and launching yourself in a moment of despair, you roll in the abyss. In such a case . . . the part of wisdom as well as of courage is to *believe what is in the line of your needs*, for only by the belief is the need fulfilled.

You may know successful people who doubt them-selves—who experience stage fright, low self-worth, and underestimation of their skills. But they *do* take the leap. They may be humble, insecure, or uncertain, but they *act.* The greatest tragedies I see in business, the arts, and relationships occur when people are so frightened of failure, disappointment, or humiliation that they delay acting to the point where they invite what they fear. Or they dilute their efforts with so much hedging that they reduce their potency and the faith that others have in them. This is the Oedipus riddle to which I referred earlier.

I once worked with a memoirist who was on the brink of writing a truly compelling book. Little by little, however, he subtracted facts—a date here, a locale there—to avoid the risk of exposure. The book gradually became less than it could have been. If he had charged ahead without fear—which every good artist must do—his book would be a genre classic today. I have seen this happen other times. An author of an addiction-recovery memoir hedged about including a chapter about a dramatic confrontation with a New Age shaman. After agreeing to keep it in, he reversed himself. Out it went. The book's quality dropped a letter grade, in my estimation. The same can occur when you shy away from a bold title. I once published a writer who came up with a wickedly good title for a collection of his essays. We both smiled over it. I committed to publishing the book. He later feared the title seemed too negative and changed it to something limp and bland. The book failed.

Avoidance, dithering, hedging, or half-measures are, in some ways, worse than never committing to a project at all. I have almost never seen a failure result from a full-throated effort. Or, if the effort did fail, it was the kind of failure that brought something great in its wake, such as a powerful lesson or a retooled project. Any fruitless failure that I have ever witnessed grew from tepidness of effort.

The subtitle of this chapter comes from a literary agent I once knew. After putting book proposals on the market she asked for offers very quickly and generally closed the sale soon after. Asked why she moved so fast she said, "Time dissipates energy." I've never forgotten it.

Napoleon Hill identified swiftness in decision-making as one of the core augurs of success. This does not mean neglecting research or preparation. I once knew a hugely successful hedge fund manager who engaged in prodigious amounts of research. He never accepted numbers or facts secondhand but insisted on gathering his own data. This investor once hired his own engineer to surreptitiously take a core sample from an oil field. He threw away company portfolios and did not attend rollout events for public stock offerings. He wanted "out-of-box" information as he put it before that phrase got overused. But once he had his data he acted decisively. Another of his rules: "If it's not a yes, it's a no." You either want to move on something or you do not. Likewise, when some-one gives you a "maybe" on a project, social date, or anything that matters, they are likely delivering a slow-motion no.

Some people say that moving quickly is a matter of instinct. In certain cases instinct has its value. When you are walking down a dark street and hear footsteps a little too closely behind you, your instinct is that there's trouble. That's probably healthy. If you are too embarrassed to turn around, cross the street, or run away, you may face a crisis.

In relationships, too, instinct is valid—but only if you are willing to heed it. Few of us are. A friend once wisely said that you learn everything you need to know about someone in the first 10 minutes of a first date. You then spend the rest of your time with that person living out what you've already learned. You may spot traits that you know are trouble but you willfully overlook. If someone is "too nice" that can be a warning sign. I've met people who offered me jobs, money, and office space within the first hour of knowing them. I later regretted not trusting my instincts about their solidity. Usually people who try to lure you in are concealing something about their fitness.

A lot of what we call instinct (or intuition) is emotion. Emotional sensations are useful because emotions, linked to safety and satiety, work faster than intellect, which depends on information rather than sensation. Hence, emotions can be deceiving or revealing. Emotions are not rational. That does not mean they are wrong. But we must know *which* emotions we are heeding: desire and suspicion are equally strong and valid. But not when they are part of neurotic patterns. Becoming familiar with your emotional patterns or repeat-loop behaviors is part of knowing when to trust your emotions and which ones to trust.

One of my worst traits is emotional paranoia—not of a conspiratorial kind but of a milder sort, in which an unreturned email or phone call sets me on a spiral of feeling rejected. This is probably due to an incomplete emotional connection in childhood. That is at the root of most people's insecurities. I work hard to watch for this trait in myself, and I seek reality checks from friends and colleagues so that I do not leap to rash judgments.

An old-school journalist once said: "Good news never travels slowly." He maintained that people rush to share good news and dither over bad. Hence, not hearing back is a red flag, in his view. I once embraced his principle too readily and too radically. Eventually a friend persuaded me that there are many projects—and many yeses—that take shape slowly because people are gathering information, or are entangled in issues other than the one I care about. Before generalizing, it is important to know your own patterns and prejudices.

*   *   *

Indulging in flighty ideas is perhaps the worst kind of dithering because it disguises itself. I was once working with a talented writer who was delaying the start of his book. He called one day and asked whether I thought he should write the book in all dialogue, like an oral history. The idea stuck me as absurd. It was contrary to the straightforward narrative of his proposal. He was trying to avoid starting his book. I told him so and he thankfully moved off of it. Watch out for that kind of thing in your work habits. Odd ideas are a device to delay what needs doing. I am not trying to discourage experimentation. But if an idea is way off base from your starting point, or if it puts you into radically untested territory while the clock is ticking, scrutinize the idea to ensure that it's not just task-aversion.

A colleague once told me that mythologist Joseph Campbell said about writing deadlines: "Well done is soon enough." Baloney. Deadlines are a vital part of planning, budgeting, and structuring. If you don't want to meet them don't cash the advance. If you accept backing prior to completion you have an obligation to honor timing. You must respect your backers and colleagues.

I didn't want to compromise with my previous book, *The Miracle Club*. So I completed the full manuscript before I sold it, with the proviso that I would not make structural changes and I would accept only the lightest copyedit. I wasn't being a diva but after many years as a writer and editor I know the weaknesses of this process, and I knew what I had accomplished with my book. (Copyediting as a field did not exist in American publishing houses until the 1950s; in my view it often burdens skilled writers with superfluous and overbearing changes, flattening out stylistic choices and substituting random terms for carefully selected ones.) That way I wasn't taking anyone's money without full disclosure. One publisher requested changes I didn't want to make. I left and went to another.

A final word about deadlines: If you are experiencing a general problem with timing, *take action*. Talk to your backers, clients, or employer and work it out together. Nothing is worse, or more deteriorative of a professional relationship, than dodging calls, emails, or texts, or waiting until the last minute to request an extension. People who ask for extensions on or around due date usually haven't even gotten started. If your work is underway you generally have a good sense of how it's going. But if you ask for an extension only after or near deadline, it generally means you haven't laid the foundations. Don't be that person.

*   *   *

It is difficult to overemphasize the importance of keeping your word, and doing so expeditiously, without being forced, reminded, or cajoled. Never commit the ultimate sin of flat-out breaking your word. If you do, do not deny it through subject-changing excuses, which is the near-immediate default for many of us. People dramatize their errors, sometimes for a lifetime, without simply conceding that they didn't live up to what they were supposed to do.

Let me tell you the real cost when you do not keep your word. Let me tell you what your spouse, coworkers, friends, boyfriend or girlfriend will never fully say. When your words and deeds do not match people *lose faith in you.* And once they lose faith in you, they see everything that you do through that prism, fairly or not. That judgment virtually never gets reversed. You may continue in contact—you may stay together in the here and now—but you will not be viewed as a trusted counterpart. And more likely than not, the friendship or relationship will end. The ending may arrive because of an ancillary conflict, but that outcome is a result of what I have just described.

When you needlessly delay, procrastinate, dither, or avoid you are, on some level, breaking your bond with another person. This could be your boss, your significant other, your children, or other vital people in your life. There is a ledger in which this is noted, even if it is not stated. At various times I've had difficulties with smoking. I knew it had to end. As I recount in the next chapter, someone who I love made this health necessity clear to me. One night in Puerto Rico in December 2019 I took my last drag on a cigarette. I stopped cold turkey. I knew that not doing so would not only compromise my health (I am more frightened of impaired living than I am of dying) but would also compromise my relationship—that is, my ability to keep my word in my partner's eyes.

The Talmud says that the most important title in life is a "good name." It is something that only you can maintain or squander. It is the one personal resource that is irreplaceable, aside from life itself.

HABIT 10

VITALITY

---

*What you neglect now
will take all your attention later.*

The key to bodily vitality—and a not inconsiderable degree of mental and emotional vitality— is learning to befriend discomfort. This is at the heart of resistance training. The more we place ourselves in situations of physical resistance, including walking, running, biking, lifting, digging, climbing, and so on, the stronger and more resilient we are, barring physical injury or over-taxation.

A spiritual teacher once told me that after people attain some degree of physical or financial comfort, it is not uncommon that "it" takes over—"it" being the thing in you that continually seeks ease, comfort, and stimulation of pleasure from sources outside yourself. This state develops into psychical and physical bondage in which the individual functions within ever-narrower boundaries. You see this in the lives of people who leave their cars running idle for ten minutes outside their homes in the winter in order to heat the interior, as though any discomfort, even momentary, must be eliminated. Or the chronic use of analgesics for any minor ache. Or chronic snacking to alleviate any pang of hunger. We get into a state where anything mildly discomforting—wetness, cold, craving, perspiration—must be instantly allayed. This creates physical and psychical weakness, which is measurable in obesity, hypertension, heart disease, muscle atrophy, diabetes, insomnia, and mild depression, among other maladies.

Michael Murphy, cofounder of the Esalen Institute, told me that a psychiatrist he knows prescribes a program of walking, jogging, or physical activity for thirty days for patients who come to him complaining of mild depression or anxiety. Very often that resolves the situation.

People sometimes joke about the elderly being cranky or finicky. It's actually a tragic situation because the limitation of bodily flexibility and sensory or cognitive decline can produce irritability and anxiety. I have observed that this descent into negativity is at least as strong, and possibly hastened, in luxury retirement communities where virtually everything is at arm's reach; where every question of climate, hunger, and mobility is mitigated by convenience. Sometimes a high degree of care is necessary if movement or cognition is impaired. But in other cases I think it leads to a lack of purpose and hence greater symptoms, emotionally and physically, of ennui and depression.

In the 1990s a pair of avant-garde artists in Tokyo, Madeline Gins and her husband Shusaku Arakawa, designed remarkable indoor spaces intended to reverse age-related decline. The couple crafted lofts and work spaces that mimic the slope and discontinuity of nature, so that the act of walking across a room, stepping over a threshold, climbing into a bed or hammock, or settling into a sitting space or swing is more challenging than what we are accustomed to, not in inconvenient ways but in innovative ways where colors, design, and vibrancy make you feel as though you're dwelling in a grownup tree house. Their living spaces require greater effort from the inhabitant in terms of dexterity, balance, and negotiation, like placing items on a table hanging by cables. The experience is one of playful effort and vitality. People flock to rent or occupy the couple's designed spaces. "They ought to build hospitals like this," Gins said.

*   *   *

If you want to learn about the physical and mood benefits of weightlifting you can choose from myriad sources. Personally, I follow the posts and books of fitness expert P.D. Mangan, who can teach you more about these topics than I ever could. But I also want to discuss the benefits of resistance training to your psyche, which, as noted, is an amalgam of emotion and thought.

The physical benefits of weightlifting are generally considered strength and appearance. That is obviously true—but that is not all. Weightlifting and resistance training give you a measurable marker for appreciating your ability to remake yourself, at least within certain parameters. Resistance training, martial arts, and other athletics reflect your psyche and physicality back to you as something of which you are the co-creator.

When I was twelve, I had a slightly older neighborhood friend who was a dedicated weightlifter. He was a decent, bespectacled kid, built like granite but without any kind of bullying swagger. People admired him, even envied him, because at a young age he had powerfully developed his body.

I asked him about his regimen. "It's 90% mental," he said. It was a comment wise beyond his years. But I was not mature enough to believe him. There had to be something else, I thought; how could you stick with such an arduous training program? It took years for me to realize the simple truth of what he had said. *Hunger for result is the single greatest determinant of achievement.* My friend had, in a sense, given me life's "open sesame."

Some people may object that I am not sufficiently challenging societal norms or social conditioning when I write about topics like weight training or appearance. And, no, I am not. What I'm challenging is the *absence* of the wish for change, whether in ways that are considered conventional or unusual. I am challenging the average-minded mentality that casts an indifferent eye on remaking yourself. The truly unexamined aspect of life, and the real tragedy of social conditioning, is cynicism and underestimation of the measurable effects of an authentic wish for change. If you want justification for these efforts, look to result, specifically in conduct and lived experience, which are the only means of evaluating a program of personal development. Ineffectuality finds endless excuses, whether situational, therapeutic, or social. That alone is what I challenge.

Indeed, strength training makes you better able to face life. I've taken great inspiration from a widely reprinted article by punk artist and former Black Flag frontman Henry Rollins who discovered the life-changing benefits of weightlifting when growing up fatherless outside Washington, D.C. in the 1970s. I was so moved by what Rollins wrote (originally in *Details* magazine) that I got a tattoo on the top of my right hand (below) of the iconic four-barred insignia designed for

Black Flag by artist Raymond Pettibon. These words belong to Rollins:

> When I was young I had no sense of myself. All I was, was a product of all the fear and humiliation I suffered. Fear of my parents. The humiliation of teachers calling me "garbage can" and telling me I'd be mowing lawns for a living. And the very real terror of my fellow students. I was threatened and beaten up for the color of my skin and my size. I was skinny and clumsy, and when others would tease me I didn't run home crying, wondering why.

I knew all too well. I was there to be antag-
onized. In sports I was laughed at. A spaz. I was
pretty good at boxing but only because the rage that
filled my every waking moment made me wild and
unpredictable. I fought with some strange fury. The
other boys thought I was crazy.

I hated myself all the time.

As stupid as it seems now, I wanted to talk like
them, dress like them, carry myself with the ease of
knowing that I wasn't going to get pounded in the
hallway between classes. Years passed and I learned
to keep it all inside. I only talked to a few boys in my
grade. Other losers . . .

A powerfully built teacher named Mr. Pepperman took
sympathy on Henry and started him on a program of
weightlifting.

Weeks passed, and every once in a while Mr. P.
would give me a shot and drop me in the hallway,
sending my books flying. The other students didn't
know what to think. More weeks passed, and I was
steadily adding new weights to the bar. I could sense
the power inside my body growing. I could feel it.

Right before Christmas break I was walking
to class, and from out of nowhere Mr. Pepperman
appeared and gave me a shot in the chest. I laughed

and kept going . . . I got home and ran to the bathroom and pulled off my shirt. I saw a body, not just the shell that housed my stomach and my heart. My biceps bulged. My chest had definition. I felt strong. It was the first time I can remember having a sense of myself. I had done something and no one could ever take it away.

As an adult, Rollins captured what he experienced in aphorisms that are worthy of William Ernest Henley, author of *Invictus* ("I am the master of my fate, I am the captain of my soul"):

- Pain is not my enemy; it is my call to greatness.
- I have never met a truly strong person who didn't have self-respect.
- I believe that when the body is strong, the mind thinks strong thoughts.
- The Iron is the best antidepressant I have ever found. There is no better way to fight weakness than with strength.
- Once the mind and body have been awakened to their true potential, it's impossible to turn back.

The subheading of this chapter is, "What you neglect now will take all your attention later." I want to explain what I mean. Even though I insist upon possessing a Definite Chief Aim, many things in life, including health, money, and relationships, place a legitimate claim on us. A friend once told me, "If you don't give something its proper attention now, it will take all of your attention later." Like a relationship fractured by neglect. Or a health crisis.

Even when in the midst of a demanding project, it is crucial to stay physically vital. In such cases, you can remain vital by not drinking booze or drinking moderately; walking or biking to work, if possible; reducing your caloric intake, which does wonders for focus and alertness; and engaging in regular workouts or miniworkouts, if you are pressed for time. Even twenty pushups when you wake up can set your day on a better track. But if you go the route of eating donuts and habitually drinking or smoking pot to wind down, you will falter. Guaranteed. I enjoy alcohol and weed—in their place.

From August to December of 2009 I was doing publicity for my first book *Occult America*. I had media gigs almost daily. I considered it a great privilege. During that time I drank no booze so I could remain on top of my game. I am not abstinent, but at various times in my life—such as periods of intense deadlines or when I need to amp up my earnings—I avoid intoxicants.

I was strengthened in my resolve from an unusual source, for me anyway: conservative commentator and author Tucker Carlson. When I was in my twenties, I was friendly with Tucker. I held, and continue to hold, a radically different worldview from him. But I liked and admired him. He was friendly, determined, and knew exactly what he wanted out of life.

I met Tucker in the mid-1990s when I was an editor at The Free Press. The publisher was, in some respects, the driving engine behind the emerging intellectual right wing. It was an exciting and even hopeful time. The right-wing voices of conspiracism, climate denial, and nativism had not yet taken hold, and figures like James Q. Wilson, Glenn Loury, Dinesh D'Souza (believe me, he was a lot better then), and Tucker were climbing the cultural ladder. He and I brainstormed a book, which didn't work out, but we remained friendly.

I have long since lost contact with him. But I was deeply touched by something that Tucker told an interviewer recent to this writing—and I think it rescued me at a crucial moment in my life. His counsel was simple but powerful. I often tell people to watch for simple things. Familiar expressions translate into power through application—and only through application.

One Sunday in late 2018, Tucker was discussing his book *Ship of Fools* with conservative analyst Ben Shapiro on the latter's online talk show. I watched it with my older son. At one point in their exchange, Tucker remarked in an entirely offhanded manner:

Choices do matter, for sure. I quit drinking so I could be more successful—and it worked.

For some reason, his aside really struck me. Especially given his notable rise to the top of the cable and bestseller spectrum. When I heard Tucker's comment, I had recently divorced. And from the glittery-grimy streets of my Lower East Side environs, I engaged in an increased consumption of pot, booze, and cigarettes, fueling a bit of a 1970s–style Lou Reed existence. Something had to change. Or I would. And for the worse.

As mentioned earlier, someone I love told me she thought I should stop smoking. I stopped. Cold turkey. Because I knew she was right and that persisting in this habit would compromise my health and happiness. But I was unwilling to make the leap that Tucker prescribed. I have never had what I considered a drinking problem. I enjoyed winding down with a drink (or a few), and also drinking socially. In early 2019 I had started smoking pot as a near-nightly routine. Years earlier, I had stopped drinking for 30 days as part of a religious commitment, and again while I was working on my first book. But otherwise, I had never really been clean.

In time, Tucker's observation started resonating with me more and more. I knew that I, in my own way, wanted the same thing that he wanted: success. I also needed to earn more. I wanted to perform at my peak. I wanted to live out my Definite Chief Aim. I knew that I possessed certain tools. One that I could grasp instantly was what he had prescribed: no drinking. From past experience, I already knew that sobriety would improve my energy, productivity, sleep, as well as my proclivity to meditate and exercise. So, I accepted Tucker's indirect challenge.

I threw the stuff away—literally. I told my somewhat New Age-y shrink about my intention and he counseled that I dispense with my intoxicants as part of a ceremony. I should meditate, chant, or do something to ceremonially mark my bridge into a new, clean existence. I don't actually keep any booze at home, so that was out. I thought about simply flushing my bags of weed down the toilet but that seemed anticlimactic. So, I instead took two bags of good weed, a pipe, and an old ashtray that I found on the fire escape when I moved into the place (and that I had since gotten too used to), put them in the last of the plastic deli bags, said prayers to the Commander, and threw it all from my fifth-floor bedroom window into the courtyard/ garbage area below. The ashtray hit the pavement with a booming shatter. I had been very careful no one was there. I also went down later and cleaned it all up. I do not litter.

My productivity skyrocketed. My immediate nights ahead were given to work, rest, and friends. My budget was better (booze is costly). Money flowed in. I slept better and arose earlier. Bottom line: Tucker was right.

Next time you hear something that sounds so simple it could fit on a refrigerator magnet, take a pause. Listen again. Sometimes things may seem obvious or like truisms because they *are* true—so much so that we are alienated from their depth and hence never try them. Attempting a piece of basic, actionable advice can be the greatest thing that ever happens to you. If you find that you cannot do it, you still learn something valuable about yourself. And if you find that you can—you may save your own life.

I am possessed by a certain blessing and curse when it comes to habits. Someone close to me once said, with a mixture of admiration and ruefulness: "Mitch is Walter White," referring to the chemistry teacher-turned-drug kingpin from *Breaking Bad*. She meant that when I get into something, I go all the way. This can be seen as either good or bad. But I do tend to embrace things wholly or not at all. This is helpful (or risky) when starting habits or stopping them.

HABIT 11

OPPOSITION IS FRIENDSHIP

Failure stings—until it saves you.

---

n 1790 poet and mystic William Blake wrote in *The Marriage of Heaven and Hell*, "Opposition is true Friendship." Blake's aphorism has many meanings. Here is one: Only through being tested, opposed, and thrown onto our hidden reserves do we get anywhere. Most of the ideas and personal qualities that you're proud of in life come from responding to difficulty and resistance.

Many seekers have detected this. The Persian poet Rumi wrote, "Pray for a tough instructor." Nietzsche famously observed, "What does not kill me, makes me stronger." Spiritual philosopher G.I. Gurdjieff observed, "Every stick has two ends." Ralph Waldo Emerson explored the theme of nature's quid pro quo in his essay "Compensation." The Hermetic dictum "As above, so below" from the late-ancient manuscript The Emerald Tablet memorializes the symbiotic nature of life. The yin yang suggests the blending of opposites.

It is a fundamental truth: Life is a polarity. It is also a whole.

The traits that you most value in yourself—maturity, perseverance, self-sufficiency—grow from times when you are challenged, frustrated, or blocked. I recall painful episodes, including betrayals, calumny, loss of cherished projects, which made me clearer, stronger, and more capable. I wouldn't want to repeat such experiences. But I also wouldn't want to have not gone through them.

It is only when pressed by opposition that we grow. If you didn't suffer you would remain a mental and emotional child. This may be the esoteric meaning behind the expulsion from Eden. Friction is both the cause and the price of growth.

Obviously you've come to this book because you wish to succeed, broadly defined. But setbacks and failures are as basic as seasonal cycles. And they are equally purposeful.

Even the sting of foolish criticism or the edge of an insult can make you stronger. Perhaps your detractor ("Opposition is true Friendship") has identified a weak spot, which your friends are too kind to voice. We are conventionally told to ignore bullies and their provocations. I reject that advice. First off, it is impossible; I regard it as the ultimate cliché in self-development. Second, your adversary, cruel and unreasonable as he may be, may find a cleft in your armor. Resolve to fortify that gap. Use every resource you possess. Seen on the sliding scale of polarity, friendship and adversity cosmically mirror and complement each other.

When facing a personal crisis, either chronic or situational, I believe that insight does not always produce change. In fact, psychological insight often occurs without change. A parched person needs water. Opposition is a help when it drives you toward immediate and sustainable solutions, wherever they may be found, and whether psychological, physical, spiritual, medical, financial, relational, or pharmaceutical. There appears a false notion in some precincts of alternative spirituality that taking a pill is somehow cheating. What supports that point of view? A solution is often multifaceted, just as a problem is often complex. Why remove a potentially vital stake from the tent? One particular step toward resolution does not preclude other steps. Is our society overmedicated, as some argue? That is a very individualized question. I believe that all kinds of possibilities work in concert and I wish to see none of them culturally stigmatized.

New Thought pioneer Joseph Murphy made a bold claim: "All your frustration is due to unfulfilled desire." In many regards, Murphy's statement is opposed by most forms of Eastern and Western religion. Much of Eastern spirituality, including Hinduism and Buddhism, teaches that the individual must become free of attachments, and only then will he or she experience life in its fullness. The Judeo-Christian faiths teach that the individual must, through the tempering of base desires, enter right alignment with the Divine, and thus, in Christian terms, be saved, or in Jewish terms be of proper service to God.

Murphy and other New Thought teachers, especially Neville Goddard, taught that we are, above all, beings of expressiveness—and that the full uses of the creative faculty of thought can deliver us to states that we wish to enter, whatever they may be. This, Murphy taught, is humanity's birthright. I stand with Murphy's approach. At the same time, I place far greater emphasis on physical limits than he did. I also believe in *acting* in the face of opposition. I believe in both the causative nature of thought and in the possibilities of the individual to construct his own persona and environment within the physical parameters we experience. This is among the meanings of the aforementioned Hermetic dictum, "As above, so below." In Judeo-Christian scripture this principle is rendered, "God created man in his own image."

Opposition is a summons to solution. And solution is what we are after if we're frank with ourselves.

In the first chapter I described my decision to leave my first job in daily journalism after I blew an opportunity. It was a tough but profoundly helpful trial. Another trial, small but deeply felt, led to the development of a key exercise in this book.

In fall of 2018, I was invited to Boulder, Colorado, to take part in a television show. When I arrived it was snowy and cold. A producer had asked me out to dinner that night with the shoot the next day. I happily agreed. Before meeting her I had a drink or two at the hotel bar and then walked across the street for dinner. We had a nice time, talked about various projects and possibilities (none came to pass)—and put away a lot of alcohol. Too much. I said goodnight and made the thankfully short walk back to my hotel. I got upstairs and dropped into the kind of exhausted but fitful sleep that accompanies excessive drinking.

I woke up headachy to snow outside and an impending 11:30 a.m. call time awaiting me at the studio. My energy was low and I felt depressed—also common accompaniments to a hangover. I cursed myself for drinking too much.

Accompanying my low-grade depression was a nagging sense of anxiety. I found myself ruminating over past projects that didn't work out, current ones that I felt were unsteady, and the questionable state of my marriage, which was in the process of coming apart. In particular, I felt stymied on one issue that I was worried would get in the way of my future happiness. That snowy, gloomy morning actually moved me to devise the 10-Day Miracle Challenge, which I described in chapter three.

I asked for something very personal that day. And it reached me. But it arrived in a manner that was wholly unexpected (and, by some measures, even ordinary); nonetheless, what transpired filled the *condition* I was seeking. It solidified my faith in the possibility of this exercise. We conventionally believe that we need a specific thing in order to be happy or satisfied; but what we really need is a condition or a change of environment, situation, or relationship. Hence, it is vital to be specific about what is *needed*, but not to be hung up on a one-and-only solution.

Without feelings of melancholy and gloom I never would have devised a technique that has been of great help to many people and to me. Life often functions this way. Effectiveness arrives only when we're forced out of the Garden and must till the soil on our own. That's when we expand our reach.

You may find that a certain type of exile is imposed upon you: when you are in an organization where the path to leadership, promotion, expansion, or rank is blocked, perhaps by an existing leader who does not want to give way. I've known the pain of feeling stuck that way. In past years, I tried to resolve it by doing my absolute best and assuming that colleagues would look to me for natural guidance. My ideals crashed on the rocks of reality. You remember the story about the channeler and the press release? Most employees sidle up to whomever signs their paycheck and vacation requests and have zero interest in being mentored. At the same time, your path to leadership is never really blocked.

Leadership and initiative are essentially the same. Initiative means doing what is necessary without be told or even rewarded. Any manager, director, editor, officer, or supervisor who is feckless or apathetic—who will not go the extra distance to improve a service, product, or outcome—is not a leader, and never will be. Leadership is not a title, audience, or constituency, but an act.

A leader is by definition the best-informed and most capable person in any operation, whatever his or her rank. Although I do not view Napoleon Bonaparte as a model of statesmanship, I've always been touched by the passage that Ralph Waldo Emerson attributed to the French conqueror in his 1860 essay "Success":

> "There is nothing in war," said Napoleon, "which I cannot do by my own hands. If there is nobody to make gunpowder, I can manufacture it. The gun-carriages I know how to construct. If it is necessary to make cannons at the forge, I can make them. The details of working them in battle, if it is necessary to teach, I shall teach them. In administration, it is I alone who have arranged the finances, as you know."

A real leader never asks subordinates to do something that he is unwilling to do. A leader is not above cleaning up a mess, broadly defined—whether his own or another's. A leader does not find ways to be out of the room or unavailable at a time of reckoning for a mistake or mishap.

A leader also acts decisively. "Any reasonable order in an emergency is better than no order," Major C.A. Bach famously told a graduating class of officers at Wyoming's Fort Sheridan in 1917. Life favors action. To dither, in matters large or small, is to virtually guarantee defeat. To act decisively may risk defeat—but the better part of risk is deliverance.

A leader also must know who works for him. There is no one-size-fits-all approach to motivation, reward, or correction. I once knew a supervisor who sought to avert conflict by issuing blanket demands, instructions, and credit to everyone—willfully ignoring differences in people's reliability, output, and work styles, and thus sidestepping the question of who was or wasn't contributing, and what support, recognition, or correction each person needed. That is avoidance of leadership.

In short, there is no such thing as leadership in itself. Rather, leadership is a label that we apply to responsibility and reliability—whether or not it comes with a title.

People often ask how I am able to write so many books, articles, and deliver regular talks. As noted earlier, one reader even asked me "with all due respect" (always beware of that statement) if I use ghostwriters. There are many reasons for my output as a writer and speaker. Passion is chief among them. Desire for self-expression is another. Sheer enjoyment is a big factor. Financial need is a consideration. (That's another area where life's demands on us often produce something good.) But there is one more important factor in my output, and it grew from an earlier period of challenge, which I wouldn't trade for anything.

For several years in my work as an editor I felt compelled to publish large numbers of books in order to keep my imprint financially afloat. I used to post a yellow sticky note marked "BILLING" on my computer screen. For a time, I felt like I had to function like a corporate lawyer for whom billable hours are life's blood. (It's actually not a bad attitude for commercial editors, though they ought to have passion and idealism too.) One season I published no fewer than seventeen books. This meant seventeen different relationships to be managed; seventeen manuscripts to be edited or otherwise put into production; seventeen covers to be designed; seventeen pieces of catalogue and cover copy to write; seventeen titles to present at sales meetings; seventeen distinct products to price, print, stock, and manage. I went to a friend who was the managing editor in charge of production. "I can't do it," I told her. She responded firmly and in good humor: "You can, and you will." (You may recall my mnemonic device: *Henri can and will not complain.*) She was right.

I nailed that season and several others in which I faced huge workloads. All of it fortified my own efforts as a writer. Although writing and editing are different, they are related, as are some of the associated tasks like writing catalogue and jacket copy. I went through countless hours of editorial boot camp until I gained the ability to write quickly, cleanly, and decisively. And with depth and integrity. Every sleepless night that I experienced as an editor and writer was the equivalent of tuition paid to my craft. Opposition was my finishing school.

HABIT 12

HARD-WON FAITH

Faith must be flexed and strengthened.

Spirituality means the extra-physical. Pursuit and documentation of the spiritual is at the core of my life. Yet I have always had problems with the concept of "faith," a term that many people use interchangeably with spirituality or religion.

I've never quite been able to define faith for myself. Is it hope? Persistence? Belief that the floorboards will appear as I take a step into the unknown?

Several years ago, I experienced a deep sense of sympathy when I learned from a clergyman that a world-famous colleague of his—a widely known minister who wrote one of the best-known self-help books of all time—was on his deathbed when the figure's daughter walked into an adjoining room and told friends and family: "Daddy has no faith." That minister was Norman Vincent Peale (1898–1993), author of *The Power of Positive Thinking*. Everyone was surprised and even shocked by her comment. When I heard the story I didn't judge Peale. I felt that I could face a similar crisis someday.

I came to realize, however, that faith does *not* require conventional belief in God or a Higher Power. (I use the term Greater Force myself.) Rather, *faith is the earned conviction that you are supported by universal, unseen principles.* And faith is learnable.

Through the work of Napoleon Hill I gained a clearer, more practical definition of faith—and how to develop it. I came to see faith as *the application of values.* Through definable steps, faith can move you steadily toward your goals, improve your relationships, and rescue you when you feel depressed, stuck, or lost. With inspiration from Hill, here are the ten qualities of constructive faith:

1. Possessing a definite aim (my mantra) supported by personal action and initiative.

2. Always taking one extra step in your responsibilities and business dealings.

3. Cultivating a Positive Mental Attitude (PMA) averse to rumor, gossip, hatred, and jealousy.

4. Recognizing that every adversity carries the seed of equivalent benefit.

5. Committing to your definite aim at least once daily in meditation or affirmation.

6. Recognizing the presence of Infinite Intelligence or Greater Force, which gives creative power to the individual.

7. Participating in a support group or Master Mind alliance with people of similar values.

8. Noting past defeats and adversities to identify personal patterns and blockages.

9. Expressing self-respect through fealty to your ethics and personal honor.

10. Recognizing cosmic reciprocity in all things.

I now explore the uses of each point.

A DEFINITE AIM

You know by now that this is my foundational ideal. Since emotions control so much of life, the very fact of selecting an aim for which you feel passion will consistently direct your energies—in a manner analogous to faith—toward what you wish to accomplish. Although you can recite affirmations or maxims that you do not believe or believe only intermittently *you can never trick your emotions*. This is why I emphasize self-honesty when selecting a workable, lifelong aim. If you truly know what you want, the force of your emotions will be at your back. This urges you forward in ways that you may not suspect—and instills you with a sense of faith that you are capable of arriving where you feel you must.

ONE EXTRA STEP

The corrosive habits of fecklessness and apathy touch almost every household, office, factory, arts space, and institution. But if you routinely go the extra distance for someone, that person will not only recognize your distinction (and if he or she doesn't you're in the wrong environment), but you will also believe more fully in yourself and what you're capable of. Doing more than expected not only benefits those around you but also brings you psychological benefits. Earned self-belief is a key facet of faith. But if you allow people to lose their faith in you through your failure to act, they will constantly and irreversibly see you in that light.

POSITIVE MENTAL ATTITUDE (PMA)

I have a tattoo of a lightning bolt capped by the letters PMA inside my left bicep. My inspiration for this, both visually and spiritually, came from the pioneering punk band Bad Brains, who use this image as their logo. The band credits its success to Hill's *Think and Grow Rich* and PMA. PMA does not mean cultivating fuzzy thoughts or trying to block out the ugly realities of life. It means believing in your own resources, inventiveness, and resilience as a sacred personal code.

LEARNING FROM ADVERSITY

As explored previously, the principle of learning from failure isn't a cloying bromide. It is a hard-won ethic. The difference between giving up and pushing on—which is to say, possessing faith—rests largely on your ability to review setbacks and disappointments, and to starkly search for what such episodes can teach you. I have almost never failed to find a lesson in disappointment, even if the emotional sting lingers. Sometimes it takes me a week or more to get past the emotional letdown of a temporary failure. But when the setback occurs I immediately review what I can do better in future episodes. Did I overlook warning signs? Could I have been more patient in devising and presenting my plans? Did I do enough to accommodate the needs of other people involved? Did I cut corners?

DAILY MEDITATION

Sometimes we work so hard at empirical tasks that we neglect our sense of larger vision. It is vital to pause at least once a day—and ideally more—to remind yourself of your aim and your ultimate destination. I have written my definite aim into a document and coupled it with a personal coat of arms. Several times a day, I stop what I am doing and revisit that written aim and image. I also think of my aim when I am drifting to sleep at night and waking in the morning. I meditate on my aim and visualize its achievement. Be sure that you never neglect vision and meditation; they are expressions and fortifications of faith.

INFINITE INTELLIGENCE

I believe that all people are inlets of Infinite Intelligence—a universal, non-localized intellect in which we all take part. The ancient Greeks called it *Nous*. Ralph Waldo Emerson called it the Over-Soul. New Thought writers sometimes call it Infinite Mind. Whatever language you use, the principle is that Infinite Intelligence is a storehouse of intuition, insight, and epiphanies. Your wellspring of intellect runs deeper and contains greater resources than you realize. However you approach the topic, be assured that you possess fuller mental reserves than are apparent. Often these reserves reach you after dedicating yourself to a chosen task to the point of mental and physical exhaustion—and then taking a rest, or allowing yourself downtime, recreation, meditation, a nap, or night's sleep.

MASTER MIND ALLIANCE

When you enter a twelve-step or support group—sometimes called a Master Mind alliance—you benefit from the practical advice, solidarity, and ethical support of all the members of your group. But something further is at work. Experience has taught me that an additional force settles over the proceedings of a harmonious support or Master Mind group. Each member, like marathon runners urged on by teammates, gains an added sense of energy, mental acuity, resolve, and enthusiasm. I believe this phenomenon is Infinite Intelligence localized.

SELF-INVENTORY

This principle relates to the earlier observation about learning from setbacks or adversity. You must not flagellate yourself but at the same time must be starkly frank about identifying your weaknesses and strengths, and how they have played out in specific episodes. For example, one of my weaknesses is impatience. I sometimes expect people to respond more quickly than they are able, especially when my enthusiasm (which tends to be a strength) runs high-octane. I suspect that my trait of impatience has sometimes earned me a "no" that would've been a "yes" if I could have been more mellow and allowed another party the time needed to reflect on a pitch or a proposal. This kind of act is always available to you. It will build your faith that you're not operating under star-crossed circumstances or bad luck, but that everything you do can be improved and strengthened.

SELF-RESPECT

In business and collaboration I urge plain dealing, transparency, and zero mind games. Such practices not only give you a reputation for accountability, and help you attract collaborators, backers, and supporters, but they also improve your sense of self-respect. Many people complain that they suffer from poor self-image. Always remember that self-respect is conditioned not only by your early environment but also by your *day-to-day conduct*. A single act of abstaining from gossip or trash talk, or of accepting the blame and making something right when it goes awry, or of going the extra distance for a friend, client, or loved one helps you stand more fully erect. This sense of self-respect not only makes you more personally magnetic but creates a symbiosis of faith—both that which you have in yourself and that which others have in you.

HUMAN ONENESS

I attempt to live by a code of "cosmic reciprocity"—
which is fairly synonymous with karma or the Golden
Rule. In short, I believe that all of life is ultimately
whole, and that my actions return to me, either quickly
or eventually. This principle, above all others, strength-
ens my faith in the symmetry of existence and provides
an ever-ready code of conduct. Whatever I do to another
I do to myself. I have faith in the wholeness of existence.

In the end, faith means knowing that what you see is
not all there is. And knowing that hidden resources
and symmetries exist in equal measure to the challenges you face—*provided you have worked to make
them manifest.*

In matters of spirituality, I strongly believe that we
make our own rules. The prayers, rituals, spells, and
devotional acts that you enact should be wholly your
own, unless congregational spirituality and traditional
liturgies are meaningful to you. You can also combine
the traditional with the highly personal or extempora-
neous, as many people do. At this point in my search I
opt for spiritual acts that are radically spontaneous. I

call my system anarchic magick, though it could just as easily have no name.

Let me give you an example of my path. One winter afternoon about ten years prior to this writing, I climbed to the top of a stone tower on the banks of the Charles River in Weston, Massachusetts. The Victorian-era oddity was built in 1899 to commemorate a Viking settlement that some believe Norse explorer Leif Erikson founded on the banks of the Charles around 1,000 A.D. Named Norumbega Tower, after the legendary settlement, the 38-foot column had iron bars on its windows and doors to keep out snoopers, ghost hunters, and beer-drinking high schoolers. All I knew was that I wanted to go inside. I slithered my six-foot-two-inch frame through a loose grill, discovered some graffiti left by metal heads, and climbed a dank stone stairway to the top.

At that time in my life, I had one great desire burning in my heart: to become a writer. I had already been active in that direction, but I was not young—I was past 40. I swore from the top of that tower that I would establish myself as a known writer. I asked all the forces available to me on that bright winter day, seen and unseen, physical and extra-physical, to come to my aid.

Something swelled up within me at that moment: I felt in sync physically, intellectually, and emotionally and at one with my surroundings; my wish felt clear, strong, and assured, as though lifted by some unseen current. It was a totalizing experience, which went beyond the ordinary. In the years immediately ahead I did become known as a writer—I was published by Random House and other presses, won a PEN literary award, and received bylines in places including *The New York Times, The Wall Street Journal, Politico,* and *The Washington Post*—publications not typically drawn to the kinds of occult topics I pursue.

My act that winter day was entirely spontaneous and spur of the moment. I didn't plan or prepare for it, and I wasn't reciting any ceremonies, spells, or rituals from a book. That's at the center of what I call anarchic magick.

Having been through an orthodox bar mitzvah as a kid, and much later spending eight years within a deeply intellectual and powerfully truthful esoteric order, which demanded study, memorization, physical exertion, and a grasp of arcane topics, I have developed a yearning for freedom in my spiritual pursuits. I have an allergy to the memorization of liturgy, spells, ceremonies, arcana, and call-and-response recitations. I believe that focusing the will; directing the mental energies; synchronizing your mind, body, and emotions with the natural world; and, possibly, summoning unseen forces or entities—all things that are part of traditional ritualistic and ceremonial practice—are best approached, for me and others, in a mood of impulse, anarchy, and anything-goes effort.

This does not mean that I dismiss the study of esoteric and ethical philosophies—not at all. But once you have assimilated the rulebook, or many rulebooks as the case may be, you must throw them away and dance on the edges of your intuition. This was true in a different line of work for the 20th century's great abstract visual artists, such as Pollock and Dali, who knew quite well how to paint portraiture but at the first possible moment vaulted past expectations. Metaphysical seekers should demonstrate the same agency.

Anarchic magick means that you can, and sometimes must, abruptly depart one line of practice and just as abruptly begin another. Such a schismatic act can bring special power. Beginners and latecomers to any field often become its innovators. For a secular example, consider Gaston Glock, the inventor and manufacturer of the Glock handgun. As explored in journalist Paul M. Barrett's brilliant *Glock: The Rise of America's Gun*, the Austrian engineer had, until well into middle age in the 1980s, dedicated his career to manufacturing curtain rods and field knives. Glock knew almost nothing about firearms. But when the Austrian military issued a call for a sleek, new generation of sidearm, the inventor was intrigued. Not knowing what "couldn't" be done, Glock took three months to develop a working prototype of his lightweight plastic pistol, which went on to revolutionize the firearms industry.

Embracing a pursuit belatedly—and proceeding to learn everything about it—spurs innovation and spurns prejudice, allowing you to leap past pitfalls and conventions and do things in a fresh way. This is as true in spirituality as in material matters.

I had the following exchange in an interview with the occult website and 'zine *Secret Transmissions*. It provides a good example of the type of practice anarchic magick encourages:

> **Question:** Mythology is intimately intertwined with magic, whether it's Norse, Greek, Egyptian, Celtic or other. But let's say that you don't feel compelled to join a group ruled by a specific pantheon but are nevertheless deeply moved and inspired by these deities and want to make them a part of your spiritual life; how might that be achieved?

> **Answer:** Well, to share a personal story, many years ago on Canal Street near Manhattan's Chinatown, I discovered an old office building that had a beautiful profile relief of Mercury above its entrance . . . I harbor questions about the lingering energies of the old gods.

I made a practice, for many weeks, of taking the subway to that slightly out-of-the-way place every morning and praying to that image of Mercury. I used to stand on the sidewalk in plain sight and pray in front of a very nice and indulgent Latin American woman who sold newspapers from on top of a milk crate in front of that building.

I don't know whether she thought I was crazy—there is a greater tolerance and embrace of occult religious methods in Latin America, so I might not have seemed very odd to her. In any case, I venerate the personage and principle of Mercury, and this was a means of expressing that, as well as petitioning favor. I felt some satisfaction, though no sense of conclusion, from this act.

I strongly believe that no one has to join anything or seek validation from anyone when conducting an experiment. Traditions arise from experiment. I heartily encourage individual experimentation backed up by some kind of education and immersion in the history and practices of what you're attempting.

Never, ever permit anyone to tell you that some kind of prerequisite is necessary to begin a spiritual practice—who is saying that, and what is the condition of his life that gives him authority to do so? Brush past experts and commence your search or practice now, wherever you like—do it with maturity, dedication, intellect, grit, and seriousness, but never be deterred by any kind of entry barrier.

Study your physical surroundings to detect your natural temple, or places where prayer, affirmations, setting of intentions, or appeals to a greater force may take place. I've already named two. I more recently found another in the main branch of the New York Public Library, where I occupy a research room as of this writing. On the third floor of the beaux-arts building appears a ceiling mural of Prometheus, who stole fire from the gods and enlightened humanity. Prometheus is a cosmic figure with special relevance to strivers, seekers, and snakes of wisdom. Positioned around him on the floor below are marble lampposts with cloven hooves carved into their base. In this setting, you can touch one of the cloven hooves, perhaps arousing your natural tendencies, and send Prometheus an intention or appeal for something you intensely desire. Are you willing to try this, or something like it, in your own surroundings? Or are you too "serious" to venture such a childlike exercise? The wish for respectability, observed Krishnamurti, is the greatest deterrent to selfhood and progress.

Some may wonder how what I am describing differs from chaos magick, the practice of asserting your will in self-devised and inventive ways. Well, I see my outlook as a cousin to chaos magick, but with an even greater emphasis on the spontaneous, do-it-yourself ethic. Everything that I cite here is an example: Throw it out and devise your own rituals. Share them only to inspire, not to instruct. Chaos magicians sometimes see their work from a psychological perspective; my path is spiritual.

Maybe it's a little inflated, but I'm touched by the declaration of anarchist revolutionary Mikhail Bakunin (1814–1876): "I cleave to no system, I am a true seeker." I take that as the informal motto of anarchic magick.

I invite you to run past everything you know, forget all your "respectable" spiritualties—and see what you find. When you do find something—and I am confident that you will—do not coddle and nurse it for too long. Do not remain still. As Ralph Waldo Emerson wrote at the opening of "Self-Reliance":

Cast the bantling on the rocks
Suckle him with the she-wolf's teat;
Wintered with the hawk and fox,
Power and speed be hands and feet.

I would be misleading you if I left you with the impression that the kinds of steps in this chapter, which I have labored to cultivate in my life, mean that there is always an orderly or timely payoff. Life, like history, rarely follows straight lines. I do believe, however, that through these exercises, and barring some extreme countervailing measures, the arc of your existence will trace a path of power and excellence. But there will be fallow and difficult interim periods.

During such times I ask you to hold to a different kind of faith. Which is that we grow, expand, and gain interior ability from profound difficulty *provided we face and accept it as such*. I have been fired. I have experienced humiliation. I have been the cause of pain in the lives of others. I know how it is to be crushed under the experience of feeling your identity stripped away.

These periods *do* pass; and they pass with purpose, I believe, if you can always come back to yourself in the midst of them. Return, as much as possible, to a simple awareness of yourself.

That doesn't necessarily mean that the pain dissipates faster. But by returning your focus within you are able to experience what is happening in a way that allows you to observe, to learn, and to see that you are deeper and stronger than you believe.

I have gone through periods during which I didn't want to wake up, or wished I could wake up as though from a nightmare; where I wished, above all, that pain would go away. But we must experience these things just as a plant withers in winter but is not dead. It is pulsing with life below the surface and it will reemerge. We cannot ask for immunity from that aspect of life. It would be asking for immunity from the cycle of existence.

Generativity may be the purpose of life but intertwined with that purpose is self-knowledge. To expect an absence of pain would be to expect, and to accept, an absence of selfhood. That is not what we were made for. We were excluded from paradise, so the myth of the Western world goes, in order that we may live and make manifest life *as individuals,* a point to which we now, in closing, turn.

HABIT 13

RULE IN HELL

It really is better.

The principle of ruling in Hell has been the hallmark of my life. As a young child and later as an adolescent I often felt ill at ease, locked out of the mainstream of life, uncomfortable, literally, in my own skin. I had to create a world in which I could experience power and ability on my own terms. It brought me to this very moment. I wouldn't sacrifice those experiences for something easier even I could, because to do so would make me less mature, complete, and expressive as a person. The same is true of you.

*   *   *

My three decades of work as a writer and publisher are a case in point. I have labored at prestigious places and at low-rent places. The defining factor in my happiness and satisfaction was always *freedom*. Wherever I had the liberty to most fully chart my own course, I was not only happiest but also most artistically and financially successful. Personally, I have found it easier to function in a dynamic and self-directed way in places that are outside the mainstream. Sometimes far outside. John Milton (1608–1674) famously had Lucifer put it this way: *Here we may reign secure, and in my choice/To reign is worth ambition though in Hell:/Better to reign in Hell, then serve in Heav'n.*

Comic illustrator Steve Ditko (1921–2018), one of my favorite artists, is an example. Steve was best known as the co-creator, with Stan Lee, of Spider-Man and Doctor Strange. Today, Steve's work—mostly in sci-fi, horror, and his unusual brand of Objectivist-themed comics—is the subject of serious critical and cultural attention. An ardent disciple of utopian capitalist Ayn Rand, Steve cultivated a strict ethos of self-direction in his work. He rarely granted interviews and wanted to be understood solely through his work. Steve was so dedicated to his sense of artistic integrity that he was said to reject lucrative offers from the moviemakers of his characters, turning down sums in connection with the movie vehicles of Spider-Man and Doctor Strange. (Because of artists' work-for-hire status at Marvel and other comic publishers back in the day, Steve didn't hold rights to his creations; these offers were gratuities). Steve didn't like the movie adaptations. Unlike artists who complain only *after* cashing the check, this artist did neither. Today, the shut-in illustrator who worked for decades in the same cramped Times Square studio in New York City is a legend.

This is all the more surprising because comic fans in the 1970s and 80s—and I was among them—regarded Steve as an old timer whose stiff figures and sketchy drawings (he wasn't doing his best work then) didn't fit the more realist bent of the day. What changed? Well, Steve's status as an icon arrived through rediscovery of the visionary and prolific work he had done at earlier points in his career on little-seen horror, supernatural, and sci-fi comics. In that genre his work was extraordinary. Steve wielded his drawing pencil the way Orson Welles wielded a camera: using extreme close ups, panoramic perspectives, cuts in time and space, combinative shots—things that weren't seen in comics in the 1950s and 60s. Steve's depiction of cosmic, magickal, and other-dimensional landscapes in Doctor Strange and other works remain without peer. Here's the important thing: *Steve did his greatest work only when left to his own devices.* That's why his association with Marvel was short-lived. Steve actually did his best work for an out-of-the-way and somewhat disreputable shop called Charlton, a Connecticut-based comic press, which he circulated in and out of at various times in his working life.

Critic Douglas Walk put it this way in *The New York Times* in 2008:

> Ditko drew his first comics as a professional in 1953, developing his haunted, alienated imagery in Z-grade horror and crime series. He quickly formed a longstanding affiliation with Charlton Comics, a Connecticut operation that published funnybooks to keep its presses running, paid the worst rates in the business and let artists draw more or less whatever they pleased.

Charlton was known not only for low rates but also for poor-quality printing, knockoff titles, cheesy licensing adaptations, and short-lived series. For Steve it was creative Valhalla. Because he was left alone. That was the atmosphere in which he thrived. The absence of editorial or quality standards at Charlton—a mark of unprofessionalism elsewhere in the industry—was what a radical self-starter like Steve Ditko needed. He excelled in an atmosphere that lacked oversight, boundaries, or meddling. If you walk into any comic shop looking for published collections of Steve's work (and I encourage it, whether or not you're a comic fan) you will discover that his most widely anthologized stories are from his time at Charlton. They are some of the most innovative comics of the twentieth century.

Like Steve, I have always chosen freedom over prestige. As a young assistant editor I was offered two jobs that bumped me up to full editor: one was at Dell, a popular mass-market house, and the other was at Arcade, an intellectual press that had just published the final book by one of my heroes, social critic and activist Michael Harrington. I choose the former. I simply believed (and rightly as it turned out) that I would have greater latitude at a house where the range of topics was wide open. At Dell I published the first paperback by iconic outdoors writer Jon Krakauer; a bestselling series of novels that formed the basis for the BBC/PBS miniseries *Prime Suspect*; and the first widely acclaimed book on the "political correctness" controversy. And much else besides.

Sometimes I had no choice in my path. While I was building my career as an acquisitions editor in the mid-1990s I landed a "dream job" at a prestigious publishing house called The Free Press, which, as I mentioned earlier, was then at the center of a hopeful but unrealized revolution in intellectual conservatism. I worked with several highly regarded writers and nearly everything that we published got reviewed in opinion-shaping publications like *The New Yorker* and *The New York Times Book Review.* It was an exciting period. It ended quickly. Despite some early successes, I had difficulty signing up good books, getting in with the right agents, and breaking through.

One June afternoon I returned to my office after lunch and found there were no phone messages waiting for me (a sign of morbidity). I quietly closed my door and laid my head on my desk, knowing that sooner or later I was going to be fired. In less than a year I was.

Realizing that June day that the end was near, I knew I had to look for new work. In the months ahead I experienced a series of tantalizing "almosts"—but nothing bore fruit. I was interviewed for a job at a defunct political magazine called *George* by its star founder and editor John F. Kennedy, Jr. (a true gentleman who tragically died in a plane crash not long after). One night an inebriated patrician editor offered me a job at a leading political and cultural magazine. His deputy later shot it down over a bizarrely confrontational lunch. I made the final cut for an arts-and-ideas editor at *The New York Times,* meeting the paper's executive editor in a closing series of interviews. But they settled on someone with more journalistic experience. It was dispiriting and disorienting to come so close to grabbing the golden ring, while getting nowhere. I was trying to decipher the message.

Realizing that I could not go the white-collar route of relying on contacts and connections, I decided to go blue collar and began applying for openings like any other rookie. I took the first job offered to me, as a senior editor at a New Age publishing house then called Tarcher/Penguin. I immediately liked the publisher, we personally bonded, and, although spiritual interests were then secondary in my life, I felt it was someplace I could thrive. Some of my friends and industry colleagues saw it differently. The house was considered low rent compared to where I had been. One New York publisher disinvited me to a film screening. "This is for industry reporters," she said, "and they're not gonna know you from Adam." In New York, when you fall you fall hard.

I did not care. I determined that it was better to accept an open door and a firm yes, better to work in a place whose raw clay I knew I could mold and where I could chart my own course, than to hold out for a fancier job at a more respectable outlet. I took a Ditko-esque attitude. Or, rather, I took the attitude of Milton's Lucifer in exile.

My gambit proved right. I quickly grokked to the catalogue of mystical books on the imprint's backlist and began to discover philosophies, from New Thought to the ideas of spiritual teacher G.I. Gurdjieff, which made a profound difference in my life. Most importantly, I discovered that I not only wanted to publish books on these topics, creating a serious space for quality metaphysical thought, but I also wanted to write about these topics myself. The greatest gift I received in publishing was rediscovering myself as a writer. I found a sense of mission, purpose, and, ultimately, a true vocation. If I had taken the advice of ambitious friends I never would have gone there. I would have held out. I would have been wrong.

The best experiences of my life have arisen from places where I had the latitude to experiment, to fail, to succeed, and to be free. And, interestingly, I later had my own bylines in the publications that used to review the books I published. So, that arrived, too. But it arrived only after I had the opportunity to fashion a vessel of my own making.

I was able to bring a higher level of quality to a field where such quality was needed. New Age publishing has never been known as a fount of intellectual excellence—but *why not*? Why couldn't you bring the same standards of seriousness and integrity to meta-physical literature as to any other kind? There is no intrinsic barrier. I worked to create an environment where some of the best minds in occult, mystical, and self-development literature could write seriously and be taken seriously. "You're the only editor I've ever had," author Whitley Strieber told me, "who I didn't suspect hung up the phone and started laughing about the UFO nut."

I opened this chapter with a quote from *Paradise Lost*. Now I quote from the Talmud on a related point. In the Talmudic book *Pirkei Avot*, or Ethics of the Fathers, which is constructed largely as a question-and-response between masters and students, a student asks: "What is the right path for a man to follow in life?" His teacher tells him, "Go to a place where there are no men, and there strive to be a man." Go to a place where you are needed. Where your presence can be transforming. Where you are tested by an absence of conventional support.

Earlier I described devising the 10-Day Miracle Challenge. I left out one detail. When I first arrived at the title I worried that it sounded a little corny or sensationalistic. Maybe the title of this book is, too. But I believe in making bold promises, and in backing them up. I do not believe in hedging. On occasion I have been accused of engaging in provocation, something I have no interest in as an end to itself. But I have also discovered that ruling in Hell—going your own way without regard to convention or respectability—produces surprising outcomes. In many ways, they are the best outcomes because they arrive without compromise.

In February of 2020 my significant other and I got invited to a reception for the opening of a new exhibit at the Guggenheim Museum in New York City, one of the world's premier art museums. The invitation came from one of the exhibit's curators, whom I had met briefly before. A lot of hustling and jostling goes on at these events, so I wasn't initially sure whether to even approach him to say hello. At the shoulder-to-shoulder reception he spotted me from across the room and his face lit up smiling. We worked our way over to say hello. He told me excitedly how he had been working with the 10-Day Miracle Challenge and he had experienced breakthrough results in the past two days. Believe me: this was not a setting where miracle challenges constituted the cocktail-tinkling conversation of the evening. But there it was. I had made no effort to be impressive or appealing in any literary manner in my choice of title or exercise. But to hell with it, I told myself—it's what I believe. That sincerity of effort led

to acceptance and even admiration in a place where I
once couldn't have imagined myself standing. Today,
he and I are collaborating on the reissue of a classic
work of metaphysics.

Here we may reign secure, and in my choice. Follow your
choice. Miracles don't come from artifice. They come
from untrammeled selfhood.

INDEX

ABOUT THE AUTHOR

MITCH HOROWITZ is a historian of alternative spirituality and one of today's most literate voices of esoterica, mysticism, and the occult.

Mitch illuminates outsider history, explains its relevance to contemporary life, and reveals the longstanding quest to bring empowerment and agency to the human condition.

He is widely credited with returning the term "New Age" to respectable use and is among the few occult writers whose work touches the bases of academic scholarship, national journalism, and subculture cred.

Mitch is a 2020 writer-in-residence at the New York Public Library, lecturer-in-residence at the Philosophical Research Society in Los Angeles, and the PEN Award-winning author of books including *Occult Amer-*

ica; *One Simple Idea: How Positive Thinking Reshaped Modern Life*; and *The Miracle Club*.

He has discussed alternative spirituality on CBS Sunday Morning, Dateline NBC, Vox/Netflix's Explained, and AMC Shudder's Cursed Films, an official selection of SXSW 2020. Mitch is collaborating with director Ronni Thomas (Tribeca Film Festival) on a feature documentary about the occult classic *The Kybalion*, shot on location in Egypt.

Mitch has written on everything from the war on witches to the secret life of Ronald Reagan for *The New York Times*, *The Wall Street Journal*, *The Washington Post*, *Time*, *Politico*, and a wide range of 'zines and scholarly journals. He narrates audio books including *Alcoholics Anonymous* and *Raven: The Untold Story of the Rev. Jim Jones and His People* (the author of which handpicked him as the voice of Jones).

Mitch's book *Awakened Mind* is one of the first works of New Thought translated and published in Arabic.

Mitch received the 2019 Walden Award for Interfaith/Intercultural Understanding. The Chinese government has censored his work.

Twitter: @MitchHorowitz |
Instagram: @MitchHorowitz23
www.MitchHorowitz.com

CPSIA information can be obtained
at www.ICGtesting.com
Printed in the USA
LVHW020439110820
662794LV00003B/11